Michae
POCKET
SPI

C000130200

Michael Prichard started writing in the hard school of Fleet Street, and having acquired the skills of the journalist he left for quieter waters. As a fishing tackle adviser, he travels far and wide in the pursuit of good tackle design. He has directed a number of angling films, and broadcasts regularly on radio and TV.

With a life-long fascination with fishing in all its forms, Mike has sought every species of interest to the sportfisherman and succeeded in taking many fine specimens from freshwater and saltwater. His prowess with the camera (he is an Associate of the Royal Photographic Society) enables him to publish first-class evidence of his catches. In 1978 and 1979 Mike captained England at International Sea Fishing festivals in Connemara and Youghal, Eire, and in both years his team beat strong opposition from the rest of the British and Continental teams. For many years he also organized the popular Guinness sea angling contests in Dingle, Eire.

A desire to pass on his wide knowledge of the sport has led to the encouragement and instruction of young anglers in many areas of Britain. Among the author's books are his *Pocket Guide to Saltwater Fishing*, *Pocket Guide to Freshwater Fishing*, *Pocket Guide to Bait and Lures* (the companions to this book), the best-selling *Encyclopedia of Fishing in Britain and Ireland* and *Fishing for Beginners*, all published by Collins. He contributes regularly to both British and European magazines.

COMPANION BOOKS

Michael Prichard's Pocket Guide to Saltwater Fishing
Michael Prichard's Pocket Guide to Freshwater Fishing
Michael Prichard's Pocket Guide to Bait and Lures

Michael Prichard's
POCKET GUIDE TO

SPINNING
IN FRESH AND SALTWATER

Collins

Published by William Collins Sons & Co. Ltd.
London and Glasgow.
© Michael Prichard 1984
First published 1984

Printed and bound in Great Britain by
William Collins Sons & Co. Ltd.

ISBN 0 00 411732 8

CONTENTS

INTRODUCTION

If we look closely at the three angling disciplines of coarse, game and sea fishing we find that one form of sport-fishing crosses the boundaries of each category. Spinning, wrongly maligned as a 'chuck it and chance it' activity, is one aspect of angling where the participant is *truly* hunting. A successful spin-fisherman is one who searches out his quarry, led to his decision of where to fish by a close knowledge of water type, bait to be used, method of fishing the chosen lure and the fish within its habitat.

Spinning demands the ability to cast well, placing what may be featherlight lures into almost impossible places. The technique of casting and retrieval must be mastered if the fish is to be attracted to a metal, plastic or wooden lure that may or may not represent anything that the quarry would chase under normal feeding conditions.

Spinning is all about activity on the part of the angler as he patrols the margins of lake and stream, conjouring carefully induced action from the artificial bait as it tumbles or wiggles through the swim. Although the tackle maker may well have built in a marvellous action to his product, it is the angler who determines how he or she uses that action against the current or through the murky depths of their favourite water.

The very word 'spinning' has an element of inaccuracy because most of the lures anglers use do not spin at all. Some wiggle, swerve, meander and dive, while others are designed to mimic the movements of a dying or sickly shoalfish.

Spinfishing is one area of the sport where the angler can experiment, making lures to his or her own pattern. Colour, shape and action can be varied to suit the experience and knowledge that the angler accumulates after time spent catching fish and reading the water.

This pocket guide, fourth in the Series, is intended to introduce the tackle, skills, lures and appreciation of hunting as expressed by the art of spinning.

Michael Prichard ARPS

Of all the fishing styles spinning more than any other approaches one of man's most basic instincts – hunting. The spin fisherman hunting pike with the spun lure finds it the most exciting kind of freshwater fishing.

WHAT IS SPINNING?

Spinning can be defined as the art of catching fish by means of an artificial lure or natural bait into which the angler imparts an action or movement that predatory fish find attractive. It is a fishing method for the active angler, one who is prepared to hunt for his fish. Skill is required in two forms: the ability to select the right water, one known to hold the correct species; and the technical ability to put a bait into that holding ground in such a way that it will be readily accepted as a live creature.

This is not to imply that these necessary skills outweigh those needed to become an expert angler in the passive forms of the sport, described in a previous volume. If spinning can be likened to any other fishing method, it is to flyfishing that we must turn. Both methods share a common aim: that of placing the bait into the fish's world in a way that suggests food for the predator.

Knowing the ways of fish and why they come to establish territory in any water is the stuff of fishing. The spinfisherman must have this knowledge as second nature for he is a hunter. Although, unlike the angler who fishes with the fly rod, his approach does not always have to

be made in a stealthy fashion; the accuracy with which the lure is placed is just as important. Casting is mechanical but the successful angler must have complete control of the rod, reel and what is attached to the line.

We spin for predatory fish, those that habitually take other fish as their normal food. Occasionally, the unusual occurs where fish not normally associated with spinning will strike hard at a bait intended for a different species. This happened to me recently when spinning for pike on a Dutch lake in Friesland. The lure, a red-and-gold Rapala, was vigorously taken by a fish that played easily. It rose rapidly to the surface and proved to be a common bream of about 5 lb (2.2 kg) and was fairly hooked in the mouth on all three points of the trailing treble.

Fish are often sought by water type. Over millions of years of evolution the separate species have come to inhabit definite kinds of lakes, rivers and streams. There are species that overlap from one type of water to another, so long as each situation provides the necessary basis for life, growth and reproduction.

On rivers and in conditions such as here on the Lune in Lancashire, you can choose to fly fish (as this angler is doing) or spin.

HABITATS

The small stream

Although rarely rich in specimen fish, the small stream often holds an occasional predator worthy of catching. The resident spinning species will depend very much on the geographical location of such a water. A highland stream will hold small trout but the size of the water and difficulties of fishing associated with tumbling shallows, narrow rock-strewn glides and minute pools establish that the wet fly or bunch of worms is a more effective bait. Only when the small stream opens out into wider and deeper pools can the smallest of artificial lures be presented in an efficient manner.

If the small stream is lowland in origin the current will be slower and the water deeper but again the size of the stream will prevent most forms of spinning from being effective. There will be a dramatic change in the fish species, and coarse fish become the target for anglers. Trout and grayling may be introduced but it will be the pike and perch that attract the fisher on a small, meandering lowland stream.

The lowland river

Every water type can support a balanced range of fish species. The amount of food available determines the numbers that can live within the habitat and in turn the weight of fodder fish establishes the number of predators that can prey upon them. Some predatory species, the perch is a perfect example, will have a varied diet composed of the fry of all species of fish present, small water creatures, and animals that spill into the water from the land mass. Like trout, the perch does not totally depend on what lives in the water, but it frequently does feed on insects and grubs that are carried on the surface current. This diet gives us the opportunity to tax our ingenuity in fishing with a lure that matches the action, size and colour of the natural creature.

The pike must be regarded as the senior predator in the lowland river and its presence regulates the population of all the other inhabitants. Easily identified from its streamlined shape and coloration, the pike establishes territory from which it forages to feed. When immature, they take other kinds of food, but when they have attained the size that brings them to the angler's notice pike must be regarded as fish killers.

Top left *Spinning is very difficult to practise on small fast streams.*
Left *This lough in Co. Cavan, Ireland, holds a large head of bream, roach and their hybrids. These fish are the perfect food for fast-growing resident pike.*

A major drawback to effective fishing in the lowland river is that it is such a fertile habitat. The quality of the water, nutrients and amount of water flow will establish the underwater vegetation upon which much of the life of the river feeds. Weed creates both a hazard to the spinning lure and a limitation to the amount of water area that can be effectively searched for predatory fish. However, in any reasonable flow on the river the waterweed grows as long streamers, leaving open runs between each bank of weed. It is possible to work along these open channels.

The highland river

For the angler, this is a fast, highly oxygenated river suitable for members of the salmon family. The water is clean and clear, normally resulting from snow-melt or fed from a lake high in mountainous country. The river will be populated with brown trout as a breeding group, salmon that use the river only to spawn and, in the lower reaches, those coarse fish species that seek this habitat.

Not all stretches of a highland river are available to the spinfisher. Every river tumbling down from the high country is made up of a series of shallow runs, deeper gliding water and small, deep pools. For the angler, his bait and the way in which it is worked are vitally important if the river is to be efficiently fished. As the gradient becomes less, the river slows, opening out into longer stretches of deeper water. There will still be the occasional rapids that give such character to the highland environment. At this point, pike will be found, provided the river is not beyond the northern limit for the species. There may be perch in quieter stretches, although they are normally confined to the slower barbel and grayling zones. A clue to the style of artificial lure that should be employed here is that both pike and perch predate on the fry of trout and salmon.

Still waters

These enclosed waters vary tremendously in both size and type, from the mighty Scottish lochs or Irish loughs to dreamy lowland ponds hidden in lush southern countryside. In the north of the British Isles, char and trout are the dominant spinning quarry with pike and perch as back-up fish. In the west, lakes, such as the Irish loughs, produce fine trout as well as pike and perch of quality. In Ireland, too, there are a few

Spinning for the mighty salmon on the Tay in Scotland. The angler is properly equipped for this style of fishing. Full body waders are a must and the studded boots give a firm foothold on the slippery rocks and shingle over which fast, broken water is flowing. Such water conditions exert a great a great pressure on the legs of a wading angler.

lakes into which salmon and seatrout find their way. Lough Beltra, in Mayo, and Curraun, in Kerry, are two examples of gamefish waters where the returning migrants have only a short distance to travel from the sea up into freshwater. Their spawning takes place in the tiny feeder streams surrounding the lakes. For anglers, one problem is that on waters which favour the flyfisherman spinning seasons are often fairly short and sometimes non-existent.

Natural lowland lakes usually contain only pike and perch as predators. Trout, if present, are introductions intended to satisfy the

vast increase in flyfishing, the popularity of which has tended to push spinning into the background. The supposition is that flyfishing is a more refined or gentlemanly way in which to take trout! Spinning, if done properly, has at least as much skill requirement. The new forms of

Amid the reeds and weedbeds of the lowland lake, perch and pike lie in ambush along the edge of the reeds for shoalfish. Roach, rudd and small bream form the bulk of the predators diet. Here, spinning is best done from boats because of poor bank access.

trout fishing, as applied to casting flies for huge distances on reservoirs and other large waters, can be likened to spinning!

On large lakes and those that have dense bankside vegetation, fishing from a boat increases the amount of water that can be covered with a lure. Given cover from overhanging trees both pike and perch will be found in lies close into the bank. Much of their feeding is done in the marginal water where there is activity from fodder fish that tend to shoal and feed in the shallower areas. Spinning into the shore margins and shallows can be most productive as the noise and boat activity is out in clear water away from the feeding grounds.

Many large waters are fringed with dense reedbeds, from which the predators ambush their prey. Trolling a spinning lure is a useful method for taking both pike and perch. It is a method that covers a vast amount of water, quickly establishing where the predators lie, for the pike is not a fish to spread itself out in a lake. It has favoured places in which to hunt. Perch are more shoal-like in their behaviour, especially when small. If anything separates spinning techniques between still and running waters it is the depth to which one searches the water. In a river or stream, spinning is rarely carried out at great depths. Lakes have to be fished from surface to lakebed, which can be far deeper than most deep pools that exist on both lowland and highland rivers.

Above *Perfect conditions for shore spinning, with deep water and easy access to a safe platform from which to fish. Never wear rubber boots on wet rock.* Left *Lakes can be spun or trolled from a boat. Gentle rowing along the reed margins covers the fish lies.*

Spinning for the sea angler

Although spinning in the sea is confined to only a handful of species, most of which are summer visitors, the sport can be conducted with the same delicacy and thought necessary to be successful in freshwater. Estuaries would be fished in much the same way as the river farther upstream. The open shore, particularly in shallow areas, is not really suitable for spinning as fish tend to stay out in the sort of depths only reached by the beachcasting angler. But it is on rocky coasts where spinning comes into its own. Here the water is deep enough to allow the angler to fish it as if it were a lake with tide.

Most people think of sea angling as a much heavier business, in terms of rods, lines and end tackles, than freshwater fishing. But it is due to tides, depth, the size of large sea species and their strength. However, where spinning is concerned, this need not be true at all. The same tackle will produce a quality in the fight matched by anything that swims in freshwater.

Fishing on a canal in Holland. The length of the rod gives perfect control, but the angler's position, on the high bank and skyline, renders him easily seen by waiting pike.

RODS FOR THE SPINFISHER

Rods

The spinning rod performs two entirely separate functions; casting out and playing the fish. Continuous casting places a great strain on any rod, no matter from which material it is made. As coarse and fly rods have developed, using cane, then glass fibre, lately carbon fibre, and no doubt boron in the future, so the makers of spinning rods have not been slow to take advantage of the progress in materials.

Rods have a built-in action, decided upon by the manufacturer. Roughly they can be divided into three types of action:

Slow	**Medium**	**Fast**

This action can be attained by construction method or material. The taper along the rod's length has much to do with how the rod functions. A slow-actioned rod will have a gradual decrease in taper from butt to rod tip. Medium-speed rods incorporate a slightly faster taper or are made with a compound taper, which changes the action of the rod blank along its length. The fast-action rod has a severe decrease in taper from handle to tip. The three main materials each have a natural action of their own. Cane is normally fairly soft and easy actioned: fibreglass is considerably stiffer and, by varying the taper of the mandrel or cut of the glass cloth, can be used to make rods of all three actions. On the other hand, the latest material, carbonfibre, is inherently stiffer producing a rod that has a vast increase in tip speed. The fibres fight to return to the rigid, straight pattern in which they were laid during the manufacturing process.

Price pays an important part in any angler's choice of spinning rod. Cane rods, although regarded as slightly old-fashioned, are the most expensive as they have to be made with great care by rod craftsmen. Fibreglass is the Jack-of-all-trades material, producing rods costing a few pounds up to almost the price of a carbon weapon. Often the material used is identical in rods selling at vastly different prices, the reason being that you pay for the skill of the rod designer and the producing factory, plus the rod maker's label.

When it first appeared on the market, carbonfibre was very expensive indeed. As with most mass-produced articles, greater production soon brought prices tumbling. It is now possible to buy a carbon rod for little more than one would expect to pay for a good-quality fibreglass model. Another material has now made an appearance on the angling scene, for boron is being used to make fly rods. I expect that there will be a repeat of the carbon-fibre story as the fishing-tackle market becomes more and more a global mass-production marketing exercise.

The single-handed baitcaster

This pleasant-to-handle and accurate casting instrument came to us from across the Atlantic. Without doubt, it is the most popular spinning rod used by our North American cousins. Light and fast in taper, the average baitcaster is $5\frac{1}{2}$–7 ft (1.5–2.2 m) long. The rod is intended to be used with the reel positioned above the blank. This suits the American angler because he seems to prefer the small casting multipliers. The handle is a pistol grip, inclined away from the axis of the rod, placing the multiplier spool directly under the angler's thumb where perfect control is possible. This is vital when we consider the reel in use, which does not have a free-spool facility. The handle flies round on the cast which can make control extremely difficult. The European multiplier would give much better casting distances and perfect spool control. Alternatively, one could use a closed-face spinning fixed-spool reel, which was also designed to fit on the top of a rod.

The single-handed baitcaster can be used with great casting accuracy. A sighting along the rod can be taken and then the overhead cast is made with just the flick of the wrist. The rod's fast taper and a fine, flexible tip mean that it can handle very light baits as well as those normally associated with our species. This rod is ideal for spinning in tight places, situations where overhead trees or lack of room to swing a conventional rod would make efficient coverage of the water almost impossible.

One slight drawback in using the single-handed baitcasting rod is experienced when striking to hook a taking fish. The rod is somewhat short and the average tip slightly too flexible. So because one can only swing the rod into a small striking arc, much of the hook setting power is lost. This means that the rod can only be used effectively at short fishing range. Playing large fish, those weighing 10 lb (4.5 kg) or so, is difficult and exerts a tremendous strain on the wrist. I've watched my American and Canadian friends do so with ease—but they have had years of practice!

After I had complained about the lack of hooking power on a number of occasions, one fine North American spinfisher showed me how to improve the hooking rate with pike. While using a small plug, a Heddon, with two treble hooks on the body, I found that a pike would grab the plug and I would strike only to find the plug sailing back through the air

The three forms of spinning rod, covering all the requirements of the spinfisher. In all models balanced tackle is essential.

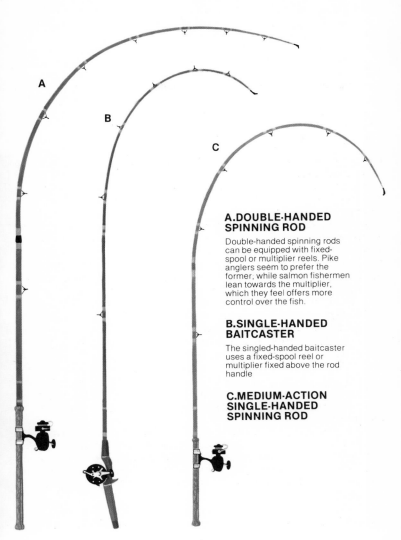

A.DOUBLE-HANDED SPINNING ROD

Double-handed spinning rods can be equipped with fixed-spool or multiplier reels. Pike anglers seem to prefer the former, while salmon fishermen lean towards the multiplier, which they feel offers more control over the fish.

B.SINGLE-HANDED BAITCASTER

The singled-handed baitcaster uses a fixed-spool reel or multiplier fixed above the rod handle

C.MEDIUM-ACTION SINGLE-HANDED SPINNING ROD

towards a rapidly ducking angler! My friend suggested that when I felt a take, I should just tighten the line by sharply lifting the rod. His theory was that when the pike felt the unnatural hardness of the artificial lure it would open its mouth to eject the foreign body. If the line was taut, between lure and rod tip, the plug would be sprung forward across the fish's jaws, setting at least one of the trebles as it did so. Although sceptical, I tried the method (which called for a lot of discipline at the time a fish struck) but the idea seemed to work. My catching rate improved sharply, especially when the taking fish was moving across or away from the fishing position.

The large, heavy spoon is one bait that these rods cannot handle. The exaggerated tip movement makes soft takes very difficult to detect and the weight of the lure puts a mighty strain on both the rod and the angler's wrist. I like to use the baitcaster when fishing from a boat. Its length and ease of handling make it ideal for fishing from a confined space and where long rods are a nuisance.

For anyone trying to get away from the incessant hussle and bustle of today's 'civilised' existence, fishing is the answer. What better therapy than fishing from a boat under a multicoloured sky?

The single-handed spinning rod

Most anglers have a spinning rod or what passes for one. There was a time when any old rod of about 8 ft (2.4 m) and a little on the heavy side was pressed into service. Great thought was put into pike livebaiting rods but the poor old spinning rod was almost forgotten. Such advances in design stem from the continued interest and demand for lighter rods made by the salmon and trout anglers, but few companies saw a profit in rods specifically for the spinfisher. In Europe and Britain, the success of the fixed-spool reel changed our attitudes towards the rod made especially for spinning. A reel that could cast a wide range of weights meant that the rod strength could be scaled down, for it is continuous casting that puts the most strain on any rod. The French, who were using small fixed-spool reels for spinning long before the British, developed the tiny blade spinner, the Mepps. It became a household name but it demanded a light, flick cast to get it out with any accuracy.

Hardy Brothers still produce some of our finest lightweight spinning rods. The essence of the light spinner is that it should handle as sweetly as a comparable flyrod. The action ought to be fairly stiff, as this aids casting and playing any fish. The soft rod makes it difficult to set the hooks, and give adequate control over a hooked fish almost impossible. Rod length is always a compromise between what can be afforded and what is right in terms of efficiency in a given fishing situation. A long spinning rod is next to useless on a small stream where bankside vegetation makes swinging the rod impossible. The single-handed rod allows a much shorter, flick-away action in a confined casting area. Rods of $6\frac{1}{2}$–$8\frac{1}{2}$ ft (2–2.5 m) are ideal for fishing smaller rivers, the longer ones giving slightly more control over fish when they are within reach of the net. The reel position should be towards the top of the handle, giving a balanced position in terms of weight and handling. Some of the longer rods will have enough handle for the rod to be used in a double-handed way, when extra long casts are needed. The handle's extra length can be used to advantage when playing a heavy fish. The butt of the rod is pulled into the stomach of the angler, tethering the rod. Increased leverage is easily gained and becomes a blessing during a sustained fight.

Three kinds of reel fitting: **Left** *The standard lock fitting, secure but does not allow the reel to be positioned to suit the individual angler;* **centre** *A fitting that gives the ultimate in reel security;* **right** *Separate sliding and locking rings by Hardy. The reel can be set anywhere on this sea spinner.*

Double-handed spinning rods

The double-handed spinning rod, always thought of as a big-fish rod, does fulfil this function when playing a hard-fighting specimen but its real value is the ease with which it casts large lures over long distances. Throughout a fishing day, the salmon angler can swing his bait out repeatedly, with great accuracy and without rapidly tiring himself. Obviously, the double-handed rod is confined to large waters, with maximum clearance on the banks and when constantly casting the larger lures.

There are considerable differences between the many examples of this rod. They range from the double-built cane salmon spinner, still in use on many rivers of the world, to a lighter instrument of glass or carbon. These rods are balanced to the weight of bait that they are required to cast, allied to a working curve that will subdue extremely large fish. The line used is also balanced to absorb the power of casting and the continued pressure that a hard, lengthy fight puts on the angler's tackle.

The double-handed spinning rod's action is very different from the

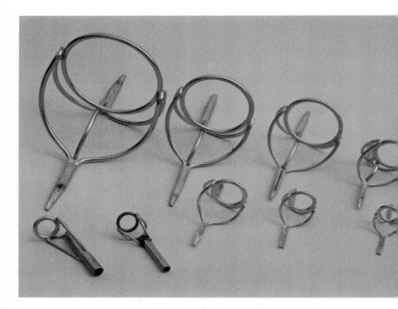

baitcaster and single-handed versions. The lure is cast with a progress-
ive swinging motion rather than the punch or flick-cast associated with
the lighter rods, which means that no action is carried through the rod
from tip to butt. Playing a fish is much easier as the rod blank is held in a
more upright position, allowing the spring along the rod's length to act
as a powerful, but run-absorbing, curve.

Various reel fittings

One of the most important fittings on any spinning rod, regardless of
type, is the reel fitting. The reel must be positively locked onto the
handle, with no fear that it will become loose during the strains of
constant casting. This means that the fitting itself will be of the screw-on
or snaplock variety. The sliding rings, often found on float or leger rods,

*Left Good-quality plain rings will provide perfect service for a year
or so. They are best used with nylon line. Below Lined Fuji rings
are very expensive but they are the best models for use on spinning
rods, where line flow is an all-important requirement.*

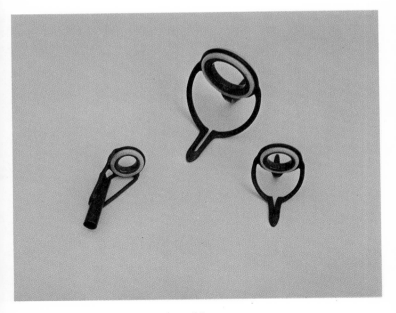

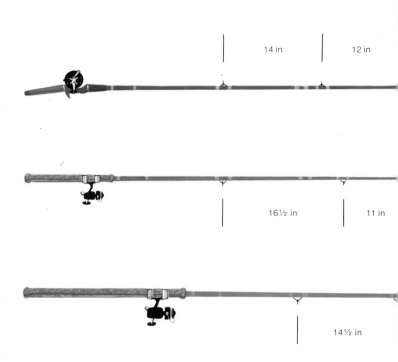

14 in   12 in

16½ in   11 in

14½ in

will not do. These rings rely on the pressure of the reel on the softish cork handle to provide security. But the constant flexing of a spinning rod will soon move the fixing rings, with the result that the reel itself will become loose.

There is a sliding, screw-locking winch fitting that allows the angler to decide just where he wants to position his reel, but to my knowledge it is available on few rods. The tragedy of many spinning rods is that although perfectly adequate, the reel fitting is often slightly out of position. Ideally, each angler would prefer to place the fitting to suit himself, though this is not realistic from the maker's point of view.

Rings for spinning rods

Rod rings work harder on these casting instruments than on any other type of rod, with the possible exception of beachcasters and big-game rods. To avoid lost fish and frayed tempers, the rings must be the best

RING SPACING ON SPINNING RODS

7½ in	6 in	4½ in

7 ft baitcaster

7 ft single-handed spinning rod

in	7 in	6 in	5 in

10 ft double-handed spinning rod

13 in	11 in	10 in	9 in	8 in	7 in	5½ in

Spinning rods must be ringed correctly to ensure an even flow of line during the cast and a spread of pressure on the rod. Rings, the butt ring particularly, can be slightly larger when casting with the fixed-spool to aid breaking up the line coils leaving the spool.

one can afford and perfect in manufacture. I prefer the standard hard chrome or Fuji varieties. Ceramic-lined rings have given me too many problems over the years!

The rings on a fishing rod must be positioned to spread the tension of the fight over the blanks entire length. The number of rings and their size is more important when a fixed-spool reel is being used, as the rings both help to smooth out the coils of nylon, as they fly off the spool, as well as easing the flow of line up through the rings. In general, rings on a rod intended for spinning are larger than those found on a float or leger

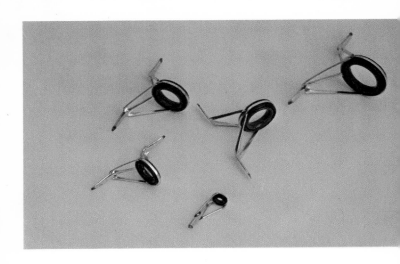

rod. Sometimes they are too large, grotesque in fact! Far East rod makers have a predilection for overweight, oversize rings that really spoil a rod both from the aesthetic and functional viewpoints, seeming to assume that the rings are decorative rather than having a definite job to do.

Inspect each ring before buying a spinning rod. Search for the harsh weld that leaves a jagged edge that will saw through running line in a few casts. Always keep the rod in a quality cloth bag that gives as much protection as possible. Nowadays, I keep all rods with delicate rings in a rigid, plastic tube. Re-whipping a ring is not all that difficult but matching the maker's varnish finish can be!

Left *Another kind of Fuji ring, less expensive than those shown on page 27, but capable of withstanding the knocks taken when the sea angler fishes a rocky shore.* Below *a section of highly magnified nylon showing what worn or cracked rings can do to a spinning line. Retrieving line round rocks will also fray line, though the water does provide some form of lubrication.*

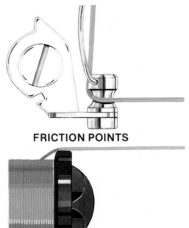

FRICTION POINTS

Above *An open-faced fixed-spool reel with skirted spool and flick closure bale arm. Drag is adjusted by operating the knob on the spool face. The handle fixes either side of the reel to provide right or left-hand action. Left Friction points on a fixed-spool reel. Loss of the casting distance is caused by the line rubbing over the lip of the spool. Line wear comes from the friction as it is retrieved by the bale arm. Good quality reels are provided with free-turning rollers on the bale arm mounting which help to lessen the problem of friction.*

SPINNING REELS, LINE, ACCESSORIES AND LURES

The open-faced fixed-spool

We must all be grateful to an Ulsterman, John Ray (although some people still insist that it was Alfred Holden Illingworth) for designing the fixed-spool reel. Without doubt it has had more influence on the sport than any other invention, with the possible exception of nylon. This reel made casting easy. Capable of casting the smallest baits yet well able to handle larger lures, the fixed-spool brought spinfishing to a fine art.

There are many variations on the basic principle of the function of the fixed-spool reel. In short, the open-faced variety allows one to cast easily *and* control the flow of line *during* the cast. The most recent adaptation has been the introduction of the skirted spool. Because the spool moves backwards and forwards outside the revolving bale arm housing, line cannot get trapped. It is a disaster that occurs when casting into strong winds with a light bait while using a conventional reel with a spool that operates from within the flyer housing.

Some reel designers have moved the slipping clutch controls from the face of the spool to the rear of the reel body, taking the slipping clutch plates out of the spool and placing them onto the drive shaft. Whether this alteration improves the smoothness of the clutch is debatable, but the change makes for a better appearance. Perhaps the most useful improvement to the fixed-spool reel has been the redesigning of the bale arm trip mechanism. Gone is the complicated lever and spring closure system to be replaced by a simpler *knock-on* bale arm. The handle can still be wound to close the bale arm, though a quick flick with a finger will speed the process.

Spinning is all-action, a fishing method where the nylon line does a lot of work, constantly being cast or under retrieval pressure. Quite naturally, any reel has friction points where the line has to run around a fixed position. Ensure that these bearing surfaces are as smooth as possible and if they are intended to turn, like most bale arm rollers, really do so.

The depth and width of the spool on a spinning reel should be chosen with regard to the job to be done. A shallow spool, taking about 100 yards (91 m) of nylon is preferable as this is more than enough line to subdue a good fish. The shallow spool will cut down on friction caused as the line is pulled over the rim during a cast. Spools should be fairly wide (front to back) so that the line is laid in wide spiralled coils. If the line coils are close, as with a narrow spool, line can be pulled down tight so that the loops become entangled and line distribution affected.

Many forms of spinning lure produce line twist. This occurs when the torque created by the spinning of the bait travels up the line under tension. A lot can be done to prevent this nuisance (which causes line to spring off the reel in kinked coils), by inserting one or more good swivels in the spinning trace make-up. But there is another unnecessary line twist induced by the angler. This happens if the reel is wound, while trying to retrieve line, against the pull of a strong fish that is actually pulling line off the spool against the slipping clutch. The simple rule is:

If the fish is taking line do not wind. Use the bend of the rod and the control of the index finger on the spool to slow the fish down.

Continue winding when the fish is definitely being brought towards the rod. Slipping clutches are very useful indeed, but they can only be set to a compromise position. A more intelligent control over the fish can always be applied by the angler's use of varied pressure on the spool itself.

The amount of line loaded onto a spool affects casting performance. Too little and the induced friction, across the lip of the spool, slows down the flow of line. Too much on the spool and the line may be pulled

CONVENTIONAL FIXED-SPOOL REEL

SKIRTED-SPOOL REEL

Left *Conventional fixed-spool reel spools (top) move backwards and forwards within a housing. Line can become wrapped round the shaft behind this kind of spool. The skirted spool (below) turns outside the flyer, obviating this problem.* Top right *The spring inherent in a nylon line retains its coils as it is cast and comes off in loops, cutting down casting distance through line drag. A large butt ring helps to break these coils down, producing a longer cast.* Right *Load a fixed-spool reel to within $\frac{1}{8}$th in from the lip of the spool, the shaded section of the spool showing its profile when empty.*

LOADING A FIXED-SPOOL REEL

Left *Loading a multiplier. Thread nylon line down through the rod rings, then tie securely to the spool using a special knot (see page 44). Below Have a friend hold the manufacturer's own spool on a pencil and applying light braking pressure. A piece of cloth will prevent friction burns on the fingers from the revolving spool. Below right While turning the reel handle, guide the nylon onto the spool, laying the line in close, even coils, but take care not to wind it on too tightly. Highly compressed spools have been known to collapse.*

off, by the cast, in bunches that jam in the butt ring. Load the spool to a point at about $\frac{1}{8}$ in (3 mm) below the rim. If the spool has a much larger capacity than the amount of line to be loaded, you will have to build up the spool with backing. This can be old nylon line or soft string. When winding on line from the manufacturer's plastic spool, use the method shown in the drawing. This avoids building in line twist from the beginning. The nylon settles onto the maker's spool, perhaps over a long period, and a coil pattern has set in. If it is wound onto the reel incorrectly, the nylon's 'memory' will make it tend to return to the coil shape that it formerly had.

The closed-face fixed-spool reel

There are two basic types of this reel, one intended to be mounted above the rod and the other below. Instead of a revolving external bale arm, each reel has a revolving pick-up pin on the rim of the flyer that turns, gathering in line, under the protective outer cover. Neither kind can really cope with line that is too thick, nor do many of these reels have a large capacity. The clutch is usually operated by adjustment to a wheel that lies under the handle housing. There are a few cheap reels that

employ a milled wheel adjustment on the top of the reel body. It is said that you cannot add further control by using finger pressure on line leaving the spool. It is true that the spool cannot be touched but a finger placed carefully across the orifice through which the line emerges will give some added control.

It has also been said that line cannot be blown back by the wind to trap itself under the spool housing or even behind the spool. But it *has* happened to me on a number of occasions when using light blade spinners on a breezy day. Occasionally, the pin causes trouble, either by jamming in the hole through which it retracts when casting or as a result of an accumulation of mud. Either way the cause is dirt that has settled around the pin, causing it to jam. As it is a major friction point, the pin must be kept clean.

Before casting, releasing the pick-up is achieved in two ways; on the below-rod reel one can either press in the releasing plate on the face of the reel or, in the case of some French models, turn the handle for half a wind backwards. The above-the-rod closed-face reel normally has a thumb pressure plate which is pressed to disengage the pick-up and released as the cast is made. This means that both hands can be used to hold the rod effectively on all variants of this modern reel.

Left *This closed-face reel made
by Diawa is used mounted
above the rod butt. The release
button, on top of the body, falls
comfortably below the angler's
thumb. The drag is adjusted by
a knurled wheel round the
spindle of the handle.* Right
*Friction points on a closed-face
reel. Some shortening of the
cast is caused by line rubbing at
an acute angle over the spool lip
and also as it is drawn through
the orifice of the spool housing.
On retrieval, the hardened pick-
up pin also encourages friction.*
Below *Two spinfishing
multipliers, the Shimano BM:1
(left) and ABU 5000 (right).
Both reels have level wind
mechanisms and centrifugal
braking systems.*

The casting multiplier

Many anglers and those who spin for salmon particularly, prefer the ease of casting and playing control that a multiplying reel gives them. Most modern reels have a cast control system intended to smooth out any erratic casting motions. This takes the form of a brake, micrometer adjustable, to suit the weight of bait being thrown. Obviously, this braking effect must cut down the distance cast, but any loss of casting ability is more than outweighed by the fact that the angler is far less likely to suffer from over-runs. Line runs directly from the spool in a straight line through the rod rings. There are no awkward friction points to create drag. Additional playing pressure can be added to the star drag system (slipping clutch) by adding thumb pressure on the revolving spool. The feel of a fighting fish is more directly felt back through the line. Again the lack of friction points allows the use of braided lines which do not stretch, so even more contact with the fish is possible. Care must be applied to correct line loading. Too little and the spool will revolve at far greater speeds than with which the cast control mechanism can cope. Too much line results in increased weight to the spool. This creates a centrifugal force effect inducing lack of braking, and once more the bugbear of over-runs will appear!

Multiplier spools should, like fixed-spool reels, be loaded to within $\frac{1}{8}$th in of the spool lip. The profile of the empty spool has been shaded in grey to indicate its capacity.

LOADING A MULTIPLIER

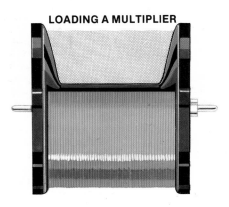

I prefer to use my spinfishing multipliers when using double-handed rods and fairly heavy baits. The combination is particularly suited to salmon spinning in the spring or pike fishing on fast-flowing rivers. These reels are not suitable for casting small baits, especially when stiff breezes blow into the face of the angler. Adding a spinning weight up the trace will help, but featherweight lures and delicate presentation are the work of the fixed-spool reel.

The angler's line

Nylon is by far the line most used in fishing and this is also true when we consider spinning in particular. It is cheap, strong, knots easily and is not easily detected by skittery fish. But it does age! Spinning lines should be changed frequently. The reader will notice that I did not say 'thrown away'! The angler should always change his line at home and burn the old nylon. Line discarded in the countryside is a major cause of death among waterfowl and other birds and rightly causes frayed tempers among the conservationists who share our love of countryside and waterways.

Most manufacturers recommend line breaking strains (b.s.) to suit their rods. Assuming that catching different fish takes place in an environment that demands certain tackle strengths, I use the following:

Heavy water salmon spinning	12–18 lb (5.4–8.1 kg)
Pike spinning in rivers	8–14 lb (3.6–6.3 kg)
Pike spinning in lakes	6–10 lb (2.7–4.5 kg)
Perch and trout spinning	4–6 lb (1.8–2.7 kg)
Trolling for big pike	14 lb (6.3 kg)
Spinning for mackerel	4–6 lb (1.8–2.7 kg)
General sea spinning	8–14 lb (3.6–6.3 kg)

Some of my readers may think those breaking strains a little heavy. I do not dispute that but in explanation would say that I have taken account of the continuous abuse to which a spinning line is subjected as well as building in a factor to ensure that I preserve line strength at the knot. There is not a great deal of difference in the quality of modern nylon fishing lines. In fact, many different brands pour off the same machines at bulk manufacturing plants. There are deliberate differences, incorporated by the makers, to satisfy particular demands by anglers. I recommend a softish line, in which knots are easily and perfectly tied, allied to high knot strength and medium stretch characteristics.

Very fine braided lines are available that are ideal for spinning with a multiplying reel. Most of these lines are made in America, where the

41

combination is more in demand than in Europe. Hollow and solid braids are available. In use, the braided line has less stretch and a definite breaking strain (usually to regulations set by the International Game Fishing Association, based in the U.S.) but it is more susceptible to abrasion by rocks and inferior rod rings. It is thicker in diameter than nylon of the same b.s. so in flowing water would be swung round far more quickly. One advantage is that a braided line floats. This, together with its visibility, is a great help when looking for line movement as a bite-detection method. It can be argued that braided line is also more easily seen by fish, which may well frighten them if they see the line pass across their heads. This may be so, but consider salmon spinning: because one spins down the river, covering each lie progressively, any salmon that see and are scared by the line have already been passed over by the bait, so there is little likelihood of them becoming hooked.

Left A sudden lunge for freedom from a powerful fish. Below Both these lines have the same breaking strain! The thinner one is a German nylon, the hairy one an American braided Dacron, and both are 10 lb (4–5 kg) b.s. The different thicknesses are apparent.

The Tucked Half-Blood Knot is used to join nylon
to lures, and lines and traces to swivels.

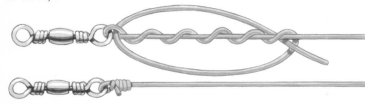

The Double-Blood Knot joins lines of similar diameter.
This knot is best avoided when spinning as the knot
can catch in rings or cause birds' nests on spools.

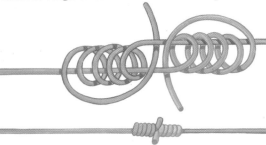

Joining new line to a spool often causes problems.
The Spool Knot shown here is simple and secures nylon
on to fixed-spool reels and multipliers.

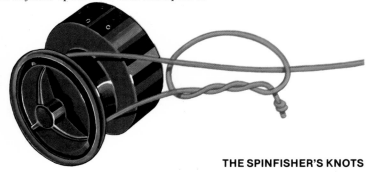

THE SPINFISHER'S KNOTS

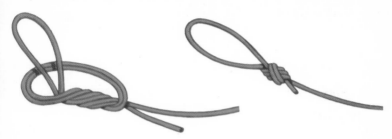

Above *The Overhand Loop looks complex but is simple when started with a loop. Below Heavy sea spinning and trolling places considerable strain on the leader section of braided line. The Jammed Hangman's Knot can be used to form a doubled leader that will not slip.*

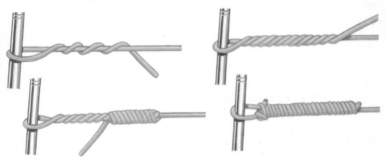

Below *Easy to tie, the classic Policansky Knot is a perfect means of attaching a swivel, or made-up trace, to braided line, which is more pliable than nylon but subject to wear. This knot preserves the strength of the inner strand.*

Terminal tackles

Most spinning styles call for the use of a terminal spinning trace. Sometimes this is of nylon and, when fishing for sharp-toothed species, the trace is formed from flexible wire. The trace performs two functions; it carries the necessary link for attaching the lure, with swivels or other anti-kink devices, and it is used as a disposable section of the fishing line intended to absorb the wear and tear of fishing use. Although some species, notably perch and trout, do not require a wire leader, I still recommend that one of nylon is used rather than tying the bait direct to the reel line. Wire leaders, made of the most flexible, cable-laid wire available, should be about 9–12 in (22.8–30 cm) long. There are shorter, stiffer ones but I do not use them for two reasons; the stiff wire dampens the action of the lure and a trace under 6 in (15 cm) long may well disappear into the gaping mouth of a really big pike, leaving the fragile nylon exposed to those fearsome, sawing teeth!

Keep the breaking strain of the leader at about 5 lb (2.2 kg) above that of the reel line. Most wire leader material is nylon-coated these days, which certainly protects your hands when handling the taut trace. It also lets us form a loop, at swivel and snap link, as the very tough coating can be welded with the aid of a lighted match. Wire of 20–30 lbs (9.0–13.6 kg) b.s. should be knotted and made secure with crimped ferrules. Keep them as small as possible so as to avoid slipping under the tension imposed by the weight of the fish, as can happen with an oversize ferrule.

Swivels

Probably one of the most important items of the spinfisher's tackle, swivels take out line twist and act as junctions between the different sections of the spinning line. But not all swivels do what the name suggests. Buy the best—after all you will not use too many of them. I use two basic types; the plain barrel swivel, usually of the ball-bearing variety, and a snap safety link swivel for attaching the actual lure. I don't like using baits with swivels fitted by the manufacturer. After use, they are stuffed into the tackle box where the swivel either rusts, if it isn't of brass or stainless steel, or the muck that gathers during fishing dries out to clog the swivel action. I always use baits fitted with a split ring only, using a clean, tested swivel from my own stock.

Swivels often come as part of a piece of equipment, perhaps a lead or anti-kink vane. Make certain that they are kept clean and tested before you use them. Select only those snap links that definitely lock with a positive snap action. Some snaps rely on spring tension to keep them closed but a large fish can draw the wire out sufficiently to open the link.

WIRE LEADER ASSEMBLY

B Tuck in cut-off end

A Draw knot tight before crimping

Left Wire leaders of 20–30 lb (9–13.5 kg) b.s. are made using crimped ferrules to lock the knot tight. A knot (A) stops the wire slipping through the ferrule. Stiffer wire (B) should be turned back on itself and crimped to trap the end of the wire.

WELDING PLASTIC-COATED WIRE KNOTS

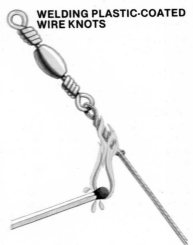

Right *Very fine flexible wire of 8–10 lb (3.6–4.5 kg) b.s. can be obtained encased with a plastic coating. This can be welded in the heat of the flame of a match or cigarette lighter to form a loop in the trace, or to attach a swivel.*

Anti-twist accessories

Over the years many anglers have made serious efforts to remove this, the curse of spinning. They have designed small swivelled vanes that act as a keel, keeping any line twist confined to the spinning trace itself, and special lead weights that both remove twist and add casting weight to the terminal leader. The choice depends on the environment in which you are fishing. Both the celluloid anti-kink vane and the Wye lead are useful in running-water spinning. They are efficient in situations where maximum twist is put into the reel line, and neither item creates too much turbulence, which would add to the fish-frightening properties of the rig.

47

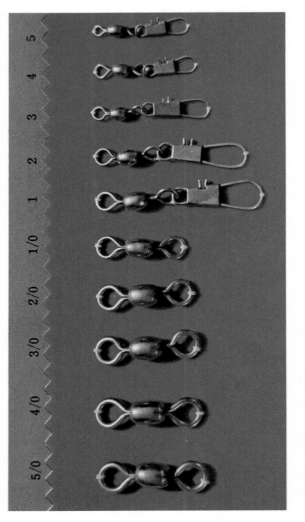

A series of crane link swivels, shown correct size. The plain swivel is a variant of the barrel swivel, with a less complex body. A possible disadvantage of the plain swivel is that the overlapping half-links can be difficult to open with cold, wet fingers especially if the size is one of the smaller kind. The 'safety pin' link swivel makes tackle adjustments much easier and unless put to an unwarrantable strain beyond the scope of the terminal tackle they only rarely pull free. The finish can be either brass or nickel plated.

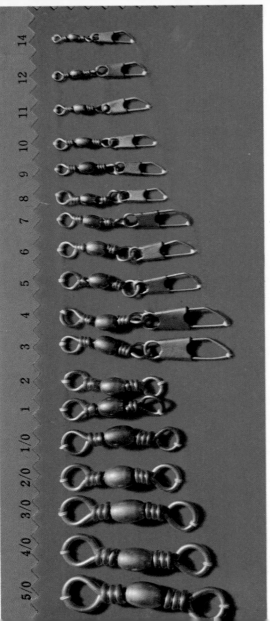

A size chart for brass barrel swivels, shown correct size. The main difference between these and the crane swivels shown on page 48 is that the link does not have the safety locking device. But plain barrel swivels are by far the most in demand from tackle shops, easily outselling any other form of swivel. For sea fishing, the larger sizes of barrel swivel are needed and it is wise to buy those made in blued steel. Brass ones may suffer rather more from the abrasive action of grit and sand while in contact with the seabed.

CELLULOID ANTI-KINK VANE

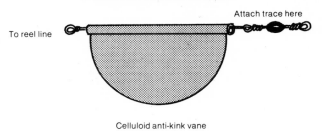

Attach trace here

To reel line

Celluloid anti-kink vane

Spinning lines become affected by line twist when there is no effective swivel present to nullify the action of the spinner on the reel line. The problem can be acute when spinning in fast water, and is lessened in still or slow-moving water. Some form of anti-kink device is essential. The celluloid anti-kink vane here is a very old design but is still quite effective.

Still and slow-running water puts less twist into a line. The Hillman, spiral or Jardine, and half-moon foldover leads can all be used. I do not like the spiral lead. The line, no matter how well wrapped around the wires and lead, always seems to work its way loose. Some anglers thread the reel line through a barrel swivel and this system works well. The barrel is far cheaper than a specifically designed spinning lead, although you have to break down and retie the trace if a change of barrel lead size is called for.

Most manufactured baits come with a split link attached, normally round in shape and generally over-sized! Alternative or replacement links can easily be fitted and I recommend the Mustad patterns to you. They are oval shaped and available in a graded range of sizes.

Blade spinners

The reputation gained by Mepps lures has already been stressed. It is not uncommon to hear anglers ask for a Mepps when, in fact, they mean another brand of blade spinner. The lure works on the principle whereby a whirling blade revolves around a stiff wire mount on which a casting weight and the treble hook are mounted. Retrieving the line makes the blade revolve and spinning across a river current, letting the

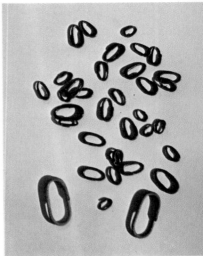

Above *Four anti-kink leads:
Wye, Jardine spiral, folding
half-moon, and Hillman
spinning weights.* Right *Mustad
split links.* Below *European
and Japanese blade spinners.*

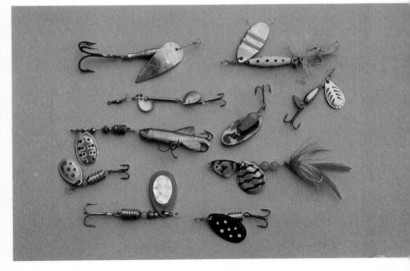

moving water sweep the bait into the angler's bank, also keeps the blade whirling without any retrieval of line. These lures, from whatever maker, come in a range of sizes and body weights from the tiniest trout spinner up to huge baits intended for pike and salmon. The blade spinner has a deserved reputation, gained over many years, that places it high on the list of successful fish lures.

There is a multitude of variations on the original concept. Marble spinners have a tassel of bright wool surrounding the treble hook. Some lures have blades in tandem and there are others that incorporate a small plastic fish as an aid to fish attraction. Still, I have not found one of the new innovations to be more successful than the simple blade spinner.

This is one type of lure that does not have its action dampened when a casting weight is added to the terminal trace, but keep the weight at least 3 ft (90 cm) uptrace away from the spinner. Take care when casting this bait, as it has a nasty habit of catching on the reel line in flight. You can avoid most of these hang-ups by jamming a finger down onto the spool just before the spinner hits the water. This will arrest the line movement, making the spinner fly on beyond any casting weight added for distance.

Spoons

There must be thousands of different shapes and colours among the family of artificial lures grouped under this title. If they have action in the water, colour and shape does not matter overmuch. The bend, along

Left *Relative sizes of Perca blade spinners, Nos. 1 to 5, shown correct size.* Below *Large spoons: top, Broadland; left, Shanny; right, Canadian Wobbler; centre, Broadland Specimen, with beaten surface, Cop-E-Cat; bottom, Seadevlet, for deep lake fishing.*

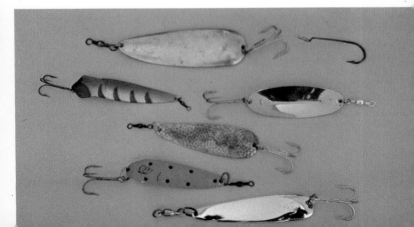

the lure's length, and any twist across the spoon will determine how it moves. Some lures have to be moved fairly fast before the correct action becomes apparent though there are others that exhibit superb action with very little retrieval speed or current pressure.

I prefer the almost regular undulating action of a large copper spoon when pike fishing. To me (but I have no way of knowing whether *Esox* sees it the same way), the spoon resembles a rudd that is ailing. In my experience, too much violence in the action can lead to lost fish in the hooking. Allen Edwards, a great friend and knowledgeable pike fisher, chooses a Norwich spoon. To him, this particular bait has all the ingredients of shape, a flash of colour and superb movement through the swim. It is a pity that some of these baits from earlier years have been passed over in favour of the present-day exotics.

The big spoon attracts me, but I have come to a decision that one 4 in (10 cm) long is the largest that can be cast without it wobbling through the air, often caused by the wind. Thankfully, we can buy baits that are made heavier, as an aid to casting, by using thicker sheet metal out of which they are punched. Providing the bend is right, they cast well and the action matches that of their smaller brethren.

Odd shapes and designs

Some makers of artificial lures blow their minds in attempting to produce the ultimate fish catcher. I have many examples, notably from America and Japan, of '*Things*', I say 'things' because they do not resemble what we are used to, but which have fantastic action. There are blade spinners that have a small fish swimming at them, positioned off to one side so that to a hungry predator it appears as if a smaller fry is getting to the lure first. Other spoons at first sight appear to be equipped with a shrouded, weedless treble hook, but which in reality is an automatic striker. The hook is tensioned in such a way that it flies out with some force as soon as a fish closes its mouth over the metal blade. Some of them work, though many are intended simply to catch the unwary angler in the tackle shop—such is fishing!

The plug

Many years ago, a man relaxed on the bank of a stream in America. Taking a breather from his hunting, he whittled a cigar-shaped billet of wood, which he tossed into an adjacent stream, only to see it disappear into the gaping mouth of a fish! The exercise was repeated some days

Above right *A selection of medium-sized pike spoons.* **Right** *Just a few of the strange oddities which, while not resembling any life form, have been responsible for luring good fish.*

PUTTING ACTION INTO A LURE

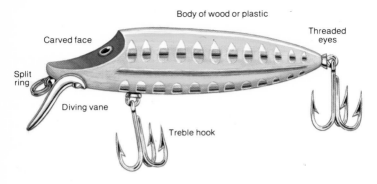

Body of wood or plastic

Carved face

Threaded eyes

Split ring

Diving vane

Treble hook

later and again the wood was taken. The man's name was Heddon and the first of a famous family of plugs, that still bear his name, was born. Basically, the Heddon plug has a wooden or plastic body, made either to sink or to float, with a vane fixed to the head and from one to three treble hooks spaced along the body.

Altering the attitude and shape of the vane makes the plug fish sub-surface or dive through the depths. Sometimes the body is articulated in two pieces to give even more action to that built in by shape and the pressure of water against the diving vane. Colour does have a part to play, for the Americans, who have brought plug fishing to a much finer art than the Europeans, match bait colour to that of the many shoalfish that form a part of the diet of their predatory species.

Wood was, and still is, the best material from which to make plugs. Density of material and hardness can be chosen to give the plug body the properties demanded. I like reasonably heavy plugs that cast well and have neutral buoyancy. They sink very slowly when left to lie on the surface. Action and sinking characteristics are then introduced to lure by the way the bait is fished.

For deep-diving plugs, a buoyant material should be chosen, that will allow the bait to come up through the water as soon as the reel stops winding. This makes certain that the plug is not lost if it strikes into the bottom. The basic difference between these lures and metal baits is that by its action the plug can search out water at all depths, not because, like the metal attractor, it has enough weight to cause it to sink.

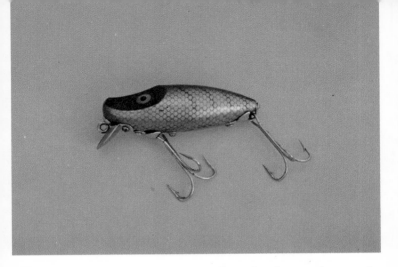

Above *Designed by Heddon, the River Runt Spook, most famous of all plugs.* Left *Shape of the curved face and angles of vanes determine the action of plugs. Treble size and position also affect the plug's motion.* Below *The jointed plug should give more action.*

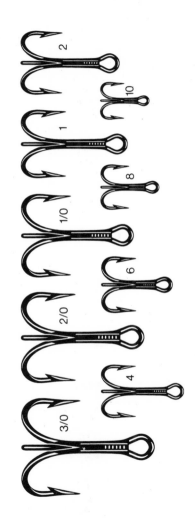

Left Treble hook size chart for Mustad pattern 3563 S; ringed short shank, in extra strong wire. They are made in sizes 6/o–14. Next page. Top Treble hooks as fitted to many artificial lures vary in length, shape and wire gauge: A, Mustad pattern 3549, ringed, cadium plated and tinned, medium wire. B, Mustad pattern 3551 A, ringed, bronzed short shank medium wire. C, Mustad pattern 3562, ringed, nickel plated, short shank, extra-strong wire. All patterns sizes 6/o–14. Next page. Bottom Two patterns of double hooks for plugs: A, Mustad pattern 9284, Limerick ringed, bronzed, medium wire. B, Mustad pattern 3674D, ringed, reversed, bronzed, medium wire. Both patterns sizes 2/o–16.

Hooks for plug baits

Choice of a plug usually depends on its colour and appearance. Very few anglers take a close look at the hooks with which it is equipped. But they are vital to both the action and hooking performance. The position and size of the plug's trebles has a great deal to do with how it works. I proved this, partially, when I decided to replace trebles with single hooks on a favourite lure and the plug did not work in the same way. In fact, it hardly wiggled at all. What anglers can do is ensure that the trebles are suitable for hooking fish. Too many hooks supplied on these baits are rank in the barb, too thick in the wire and almost blunt. Changing them for the best-quality irons will radically improve their hooking and holding power. I would like to see some development work put into the use of double hooks, instead of trebles, on many plug bodies. The few examples that I've tried have succeeded.

TREBLE HOOK PATTERNS

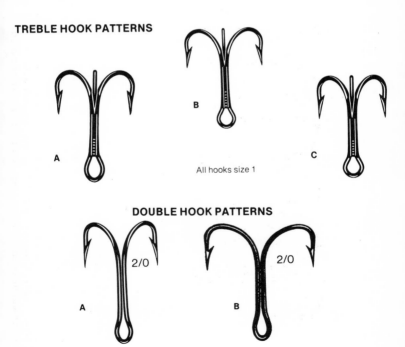

A

B

C

All hooks size 1

DOUBLE HOOK PATTERNS

A   2/0

B   2/0

The diving plug
As has already been stated, the diving action of a plug comes from the position and shape of the vane. With a shallow angle set on a large vane, the plug will go deep. A small surface area and steeply set vane causes the plug to dive at a less steep angle. Weight in the body has very little to do with the way in which a plug sinks. That famous pike angler and author Fred Buller recommends that we should improve our spinning traces to maximise the plug's action. Fred suggests a leader made of stiffish wire, called Alasticum, formed with a large loop for the plug split link to move around. Obviously, the loop must be regularly inspected to ensure it has retained its rounded shape.

Surface working plugs
These can generally be recognized by the absence of a forward-facing diving vane. The plug is made of floating material, often with tiny propellers at front and rear that thrash round as the plug moves in the water. Probably, a taking fish sees the disturbance as a swimming animal, or perhaps the propellers suggest the appearance and vibrations of a water vole swimming across the stream.

The oddities
It is no different when we come to look closely at some lures offered on our market. All too often, importers take the view that what sells in America will necessarily sell and catch fish in Europe. First, the number of predatory—spinning—species available to us is fewer than in America. Geographically the Americas cover a much wider water temperature span that gives them almost 50 different fish species which will chase artificials. A massive range of plugs has been developed purely for the saltwater angler and these plugs do catch fish. When did you last read of a British sea fisherman catching large fish on a plug?

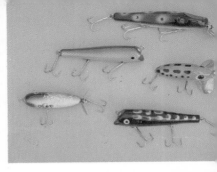

Above *Deep-divers from Japan and the U.S.* Above right *Surface working plugs rely on floating properties and face-scoops.* Right *Two surface plugs which disturb the water, perhaps suggesting a swimming animal.* Below *These lures have a smooth action unlike those which wobble erratically: Japanese lure (top); The Rebel for trolling (centre); An original Lauri Rapala lure (bottom).* Bottom left *Deep-diving plugs. Note length and attitude of vanes. Top is a Rapala, lower two are both copies of Heddon lures.*

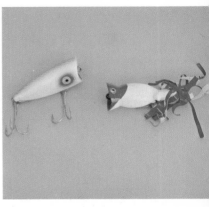

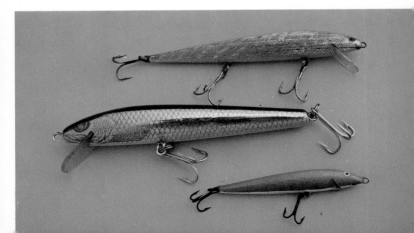

Above *These three lures make a rattling sound when retrieved. Why fish react to them is debatable, but the author has certainly had success with pike while using them.* Right *Three examples of U.S. and Japanese ingenuity, lures in combined metal and plastic.*

Above *Popping Bugs, extremely popular in the U.S. where they are used for casting to bass and other freshwater predators.* Right *A plastic-coated lead paravane with adjustable attachments for deep trolling.*

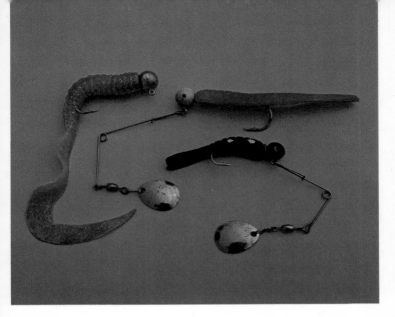

Still, like our flyfishing compatriots, we can always build up a plug collection to dream over and impress non-angling friends!

Things made of plastic

Immediately, we think of lures like the Redgill and Mevagissey eel, used so extensively by the sea angler. But there are models intended for use in freshwater. I've had both trout and perch on the smallest plastic representations of a swimming fish, and I may have caught more if I had persevered rather than resorting to tried-and-true lures that always lie on the top of the tackle box trays. I think that these unusual and innovative baits are best tried when things are going well and the fish are taking almost anything, not when the going is tough. You will then know how effective they are.

Spinning with natural baits

The oldest spinning methods are those which use a dead fish. Spinning a freshwater or marine deadbait does not seem to matter, it is how the technique is applied that catches the predator. Sometimes the bait is actually rigged to spin but more often than not the intention is to work it in an attractive up-and-down fashion. Sink-and-draw is the name given to the technique and it is particularly productive in the colder months.

Pike, perch and zander will all take a bait that is worked through the swim in a lifelike manner. The intention must be to present a deadbait in a way that suggests the bait is either wounded or about to die. But this technique is not always as easy as perhaps it seems. Timing must be perfect. The bait should be attached to a wired sink-and-draw mount, in the case of pike fishing, by running a No. 8 treble hook onto a piece of Alasticum wire. Twist the wire over itself to secure the hook. Slip a bead down to the hook eye, to prevent the trace being pulled into the body of the fish during strong casts. Use a baiting needle to draw the wire through the bait, from the fish's vent to emerge at the mouth. Add a No. 2 single hook that penetrates both lips of the deadbait.

Puncture the bait's swimbladder with a baiting needle to give a slow-sinking bait. To make the bait sink quickly, add a barrel lead to the wire mount before putting-on the single hook.

Small freshwater fish or sprats can be mounted on a fine, flexible wire trace, formed as a loop, then passed through the eye of a single hook and around the body of the bait. Sufficient casting weight can be added by means of a barrel swivel mounted on the reel line above a connecting swivel. Do not stifle the action by adding too much weight.

Spinning a deadbait

Most tackle shops can provide a ready-made mount, called an Archer flight, for spinning small deadbaits such as minnows or tiny roach, which are ideal. The bait is slipped along the weighted prong until the

Sink-and-draw rig using a sprat on a short wire mount.

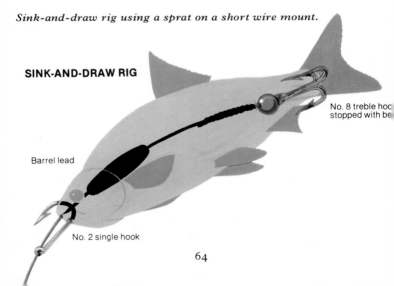

SINK-AND-DRAW RIG

No. 8 treble hook stopped with be

Barrel lead

No. 2 single hook

THE ARCHER FLIGHT

The Archer flight, a rig for spinning a natural fish bait.

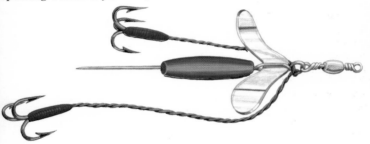

fish's mouth fits against the celluloid vanes. A treble is pressed into each flank to secure the bait. The method is most useful for flicking a small bait into those hard-to-fish places that are always the fish-holding lies on a small stream. I like to give the spinning action additional life by retrieving in an erratic manner that blends the spin with a sink-and-draw attractiveness. The Archer flight can be bought in a number of different sizes made to accommodate a variety of deadbaits. Your baits should not fly off during the cast but if they do, tie the trebles close against the bait with some fine elasticated thread.

Trolling a deadbait

Trolling is the art of towing a mounted deadbait behind a rowed or slowly propelled boat perhaps driven by an outboard engine. At first, this may appear to many to be a lazy way to fish. But that could not be farther from the truth when done properly. Trolling is a means by which a large water, such as a big lake, can be experimentally fished to establish the presence of predators. A greater area can be covered than would be possible by spinning the lake over by other means.

On a deep lake, the trolled bait can be set to fish at a particular depth by adding weight to the trace or by careful adjustment of the boat's speed. Experience will prove that it is a balanced use of both factors that gives the best fishing depth. Really deep trolling is accomplished by using a paravane that dives as soon as forward motion is applied to the bait by the boat's travel. The pull of a hooked fish alters the paravane's angle of attack, forcing it up to the surface.

Deep trolling can also be carried out using fairly heavy weights, which takes a lot of feeling away from the rod, but if that is the place for a bait to be the angler must persevere. I prefer the paravane because it is nowhere as heavy as a trolling weight yet works far better in getting the bait down through the water.

The trolling trace need only be of wire when fishing for pike. A long wire leader is not necessary. One of about 1 ft (30 cm) long will keep the pike's teeth away from the reel line. Use two swivels to take out any line twist and keep the trolling weight at least 6 ft (1.8 m) from the bait, to put maximum action into it.

Disgorgers

There will be times when a fish is hooked quite deeply or, as when pike fishing, the quarry has large teeth. Removing the hook or hooks from most species is simple but only if the correct instruments are to hand. Always use artery forceps to get the hooks free. They do not damage a fish's mouth like those vicious pronged disgorgers that one sees for sale. Probing around in the mouth of any fish with one of those old-fashioned weapons can only result in damage to the fish's throat-membranes and delicate gill frills.

Getting hooks out of a pike's mouth is somewhat more difficult than with other species. First we have to avoid injury that can be done to us by the fish. Holding the fish firmly, behind the gillcases, will cause the fish to open its mouth. The jaws will then have to be kept open with a gag. This can be a billet of wood placed across the jaws, or a manufactured gag. And once more we have to take a close look at the shop-bought article. Some makers still insist in producing gags with sharp prongs at each end of the sprung arms. The ends of the gag prongs should be buffered with thick plastic or rubber grommets so that when they keep the fish's jaws apart they do it no harm. After all that has been written about injuring fish one would think that manufacturers would turn their undoubted skills to getting things right.

Using the forceps on a pike

With a small pike, hold it firmly behind the gills, but do not squeeze too hard. If the pike is of specimen size, get a companion to help to restrain the fish's movements. Insert the gag between top and bottom jaws,

THE TROLLING RIG

Flexible wire trace

Nylon

Wye lead

The pike's jaws have to be prised open carefully so that the gag can be inserted. The fish will open its mouth if grasped firmly behind the gill covers.

The gag must be correctly placed before releasing the spring, and the gag ends must be protected by rubber grommets or thick plastic tape.

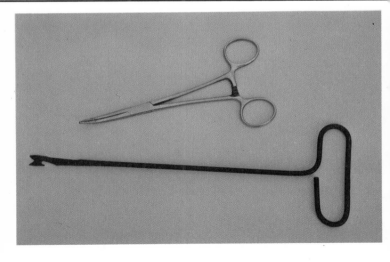

Artery forceps are by far the best disgorgers, and they last for ever. The lower model is lethal to pike and is subject to rust.

Grip the shank of the treble, lock the forceps. Then give a positive push against the direction of the barb entry. This releases the barb's hold.

If the hookhold prevents removal cut the treble into pieces with your wire cutters. Remove the pieces in sections, causing the fish no harm.

making certain that the gag sits securely inside the front of the jaws, not back in the softer mouth area. I have seen a strongly sprung gag force its way into the flesh and almost out of the roof of a pike's mouth. This is totally unnecessary and cruel.

Next, using the forceps, grip the shank of the treble hook. Artery forceps lock as you squeeze the grips together, which helps immensely in providing a positive hold. Push the hook away from you, against the holding power of the barb. If the hook is stubborn a slight jerk will soon free it from the jaw.

If the pike has taken the bait down, with the hook well back in the throat, it can be removed by entering the forceps via the gill slit. Obviously one has to be very careful. Make sure the fish is restrained as any sudden thrashing movement will make removal almost impossible. Lift the gillcase and hold the fish so that the hook can be seen. Never try to take hold of a hook that you cannot see. Grip the shank and turn it over on itself. This will free the hold. Then, through the mouth, grip the trace wire lightly to lift it free. Rarely will the hook take another hold, it is just a matter of extreme care and patience. Avoid sudden movements and carry out every action purposefully, for the fish's life is in *your* hands and with it its possible progeny—and on a greater scale the future of the sport.

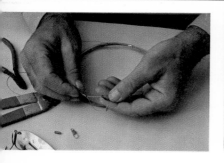

A loop is formed in the wire to hold either a swivel or a split link. For strength, a brass ferrule is used to hold the wire tight to the tackle item.

Ferrule pliers are used to lock the wire tight in the ferrule by crimping it. It is then held absolutely firm and one more weak link has been avoided.

Making wire spinning traces

The tools for the construction of home-made wire spinning traces are simple. A pair of quality wire cutters and a pair of ferrule pliers are required as well as barrel swivels, link swivels and brass ferrules that fit the diameter of the chosen wire line. The length of the wire trace depends on where and for what you are fishing. The average pike spinning trace need not be longer than 9–12 in (22.8–30 cm). The fish chase after the spinner or plug and when they take they are usually hooked towards the front of the jaw, unlike livebaiting and deadbait techniques where the unwary angler simply lets the fish swallow the bait and in so doing suffers a gorged bait.

Choose a wire of a strength that will give maximum breaking strain, as a security against the cutting power of a fish's teeth, with the greatest

A large landing net is absolutely essential for coping with big fish. Never attempt to lift a heavy fish in a net by using just the handle. Use two hands, one on the net rim, the other on the handle.

Unlike nylon knots which can slip, crimped wire in a ferrule never slips, no matter how much tension is applied to it. Any break will occur elsewhere.

Wire traces can be made at home cheaply. All you need are quality wire cutters, ferrule pliers and a supply of brass ferrules, line and swivels.

flexibility. There is no point in having a wire trace that is weaker than the nylon reel line. The following trace strengths will give a balance to fish sizes, the habitat in which they live and the reel line strength.

Fish and situations	Reel line	Trace wire
Pike spinning in rivers	8–14 lb (3.6–6.3 kg)	30 lb (13.6 kg)
Pike spinning in lakes	10 lb (4.5 kg)	20 lb (9.0 kg)
Trolling for big pike	14 lb (6.3 kg)	30 lb (13.6 kg)
General sea spinning	8–14 lb (3.6–6.3 kg)	30 lb (13.6 kg)

I find that it pays to increase the breaking strain when spinning in a river where one has to combat snags or other abrasive obstructions. Spinning in a lake is an open-area situation calling for less regard to potential hazards, especially when the fishing is conducted from a boat. Sea spinning can mean hard wear for the trace and the reel line. I increase the wire trace length to 3 ft (91 cm). A golden rule to observe is: *always* have terminal tackle stout enough both to hold the fish you seek and also to withstand possible abrasive hazards.

The landing net

For most of our spinning we would use a standard triangular landing net, of the fixed or folding variety. Avoid extra long handles as they become a nuisance in the mobility of spinning. Similarly, coarse-fishing

Unless the fish is very small, never lift it from the water on the end of the line by raising the rod. Draw the fish carefully towards the waiting landing net.

With the rod tip high, slide the fish over the surface of the water. As the bulk of the body crosses the net rim, lift the landing net handle.

pan nets (those with a round rim) have no place in this aspect of the sport. Big fish, whether they are salmon or pike, need a big net. I like a triangular one with a deep open mesh net. The fine, soft netting from which most modern coarse-fishing nets are made is of little use because treble hooks get caught up in the mesh.

Using the landing net

I will presuppose that the angler is fishing alone, as it is far more difficult to land a big fish by oneself. The first thing one must do is place the net in a handy position, relative to where the fishing is taking place. All too often the fisherman leaves his net lying somewhere up the bank. Have it set up ready to go into action.

When a fish is hooked, give your whole attention to playing the fish out. Do not attempt to bring a fish to the net before it is ready. Make sure you know where the net is. Then play the fish towards you as you take the necessary steps to pick the net up. Lay it in the water so that the net mesh sinks to the bottom. Reel in line so that the amount out between rod tip and fish is slightly less than the length of the rod. Jam your finger down onto the reel spool so as to prevent the clutch slipping. Should the fish make a sudden move away, it is easy to lift the finger to re-assert the preset drag.

Bring the fish in without a jerky motion. As it crosses the rim of the

Above *As the tail slides into the net, raise the net. Put the rod down and use two hands to grasp the net firmly. Move back from water's edge (right).*

net, lift the handle, which will make the tail of the fish slide down over the net frame. You cannot lift a heavy fish just by holding the end of the handle by one hand, so don't attempt it. While keeping the handle high, place the rod on the ground, then with the free hand grasp the handle and slide it back through both hands, drawing the fish to the bankside.

Lift the net frame with both hands and carry the fish away from the water. Then remove the hooks in the knowledge that the fish cannot flip back into its habitat!

When used properly the gaff is an efficient fish-landing instrument. But when used incorrectly, it can cause totally unnecessary injury.

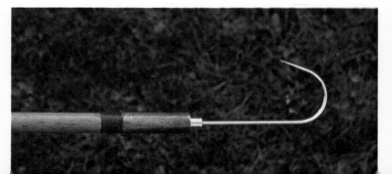

The gaff

A book reviewer recently took me to task for explaining the proper use of a gaff. He thought, wrongly, that I was advocating the use of this landing instrument. In fact he went on to write that the Pike Fishers Club wouldn't like it! I know that that band of august fishers are quite rightly opposed to gaffing but that doesn't stop tackle dealers selling them or anglers, without the care, knowledge and experience of serious pike men, from using them. I therefore offer these few words in the hope that people who must buy and use gaffs try to do the correct thing with them.

Using pike as the example, I suggest that the only place to insert a gaff is in the membraned joint in the fish's lower jaw. With the fish's head facing you, lower the gaff head below the water and draw the gaff into that slot that exists just behind the rim of the lower jaw bone. When done properly this inflicts practically no harm. Lift the fish's head and slide it from the water. Remove the gaff immediately. Never let the pike twist on the gaff, it could cause irreparable harm.

Salmon fishermen who gaff fish mostly do so at the point of balance, which is about midway along the thick part of the body. They use the gaff to be certain of getting their fish on the bank, *but* remember that the fish will be humanely killed within seconds of leaving the water.

Sea anglers use a gaff because it is by far the easiest instrument to handle in the tight confines of a small boat on a heaving sea. Again, they should kill the fish immediately after boating it. Huge fish, such as common skate, are gaffed in both wings, by two men. The fish suffers little harm and it will be released to the sea after inspection and possible photographing and tagging.

The tailer

Because of the danger of gaffing a salmon that is required by law to be returned to the water, many salmon anglers use a tailer. This is essentially a stiff wire lasso that is drawn over the tail of the fish to be pulled tight at the wrist, the thick, fleshy part of the body from which the tail branches. No harm is done to the fish at all and the tailer cannot slip off. Unfortunately, a tailer cannot be used on pike because this fish lacks that thickened wrist to its tail. A tightened tailer would just slip off.

The spinfisher's tackle box

We spinners tend to accumulate a fair amount of tackle. Plugs, spoons and the hundred and one bits and pieces that go to make up angling gear are bulky and expensive. So they deserve to be contained in something that will carry everything and keep the tackle dry and reasonably clean. Hooks and their condition, are of vital importance to any angler but especially so to the fisherman who spins. I take the precaution of drying

Left *When gaffing a pike, the point should pierce the thin membrane under the 'chin' where the lower jawbones meet. It causes very little harm to the fish. This should not be done in hurried fashion, for the pike should by then be properly played out.* **Below** *Spinners and lures should not be kept loose in an ordinary tackle box. This means that a purpose-built spinfishers' box should be acquired to hold such costly items of tackle in separate sections for each kind of lure and to hold all the accessories needed to repair spinning rigs at the waterside. The secret is to keep rust at bay.*

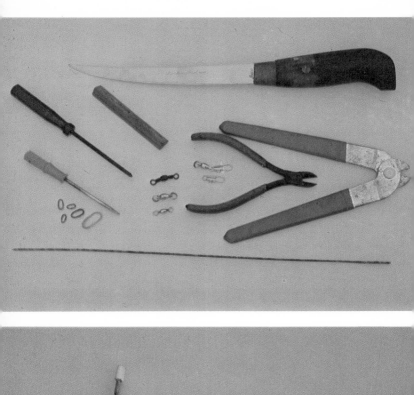

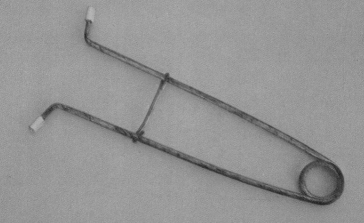

Left *The few quality tools needed to construct rigs and present perfect spinning baits: crimping pliers, wire cutters, filleting knife, baiting needle, hook-sharpening stone, and two small screwdrivers, which are invaluable when a reel develops a fault at the waterside. Without one, you may have to pack up and go home, a frustrated angler.* Below left *A gag should have a reasonable amount of spring in it, and the points must be well protected by rubber grommets or thick plastic tape.* Right *The author's spinning tackle box. It contains everything for a spinning session in fresh or saltwater, and includes trace-making tools and forceps.*

the plugs and spoons before putting the tackle box away for any length of time to prevent that inevitable rusting that occurs on bronzed hooks and the split links. Some people use stainless-steel hooks but I find that they are never, initially, as sharp and I don't seem to be able to put a really keen point to them with the sharpening stone.

Try to buy a tackle box that is made from ABS material. This prevents plastic lures going soft and mushy when in touch with plastic trays. I have a box, from America, that has cork inserts in each of the divided trays. This certainly stops the lures banging about and taking the edge off the hooks, but a lure put away wet stays wet. I like large boxes. I know, too, that all this stuff has to be carried but it is with the knowledge that everything needed will be with me. The box goes into the car or boat, if that is what I'm fishing from. After seeing the water, I take enough gear out of the box to be carried over the shoulder in a canvas bag. Entire days spent spinning mean a walk of some miles. The shoulder bag is carried easily; a box is an impediment.

Include a few essential tools in the tackle box: spanners for the reels and a couple of small screwdrivers, one of each kind of screw head. An oil-bottle is a must, though make sure that it closes tightly, for if oil gets onto lures they carry its taint down to the fish. A small box with rudimentary first-aid items is a good idea. I've yet to hook myself on a treble, but I've twice had to cut them from other people. Finally, a good quality filleting knife will make the kit complete.

After a day's fishing, try to get into the habit of cleaning reels and items of gear that have got wet. A smear of oil on the junction of wire cutter blades and ferrule pliers helps tremendously next time they are used. Get a good hook-sharpening stone, preferably one with a v-shaped trough scored along one side, to put the finishing touch to blunt trebles. There are at least three different ways to protect hooks by shrouding the bend and points. The cheap protectors work but are inevitably lost easily. I have some plastic devices, from Sweden, that both shroud the vital point and act in a sprung fashion that creates a weedless spoon, and very good they are too.

Hook points can be protected if they are shrouded by a plastic cover. This keeps the points sharp, and at the same time the trebles can quite safely be carried in the pocket.

Above *The sharpening stone, a necessary item of equipment for anglers.* Below *Coils of loose nylon which spring off the spool are a nuisance. A plastic circlet keeps the line tight.*

INDEX FINGER POSITION
ON FIXED-SPOOL REEL

*The index finger hovers over the spool, slightly arresting the line,
or it can be jammed down to abruptly stop the flight of the line.*

*On multipliers, the thumb controls the spool. Gentle pressure
smooths out the coils as the spool revolves during a cast.*

THUMB CONTROL
ON MULTIPLIERS

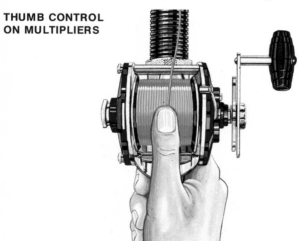

CASTING

Control during the cast

A good angler is one who knows where the bait is going to hit the water. Not everybody has the sense of feel that an habitual spinfisher develops. Now and then we all make a bad cast that leaves the expensive lure heading for a bunch of reeds—and which must be stopped before it lands in them. The emphasis on any cast must be on following through, with hands and eyes, ready to react to any unexpected happening. Jamming the index finger down on the spool will stop a bait immediately but its flight can be slowed by feathering the coils of nylon as they pull off the spool. Just a slight smoothing pressure is enough to halt the flight progressively.

Controlling a multiplier is slightly more difficult because this type of reel has a completely free-turning spool. The weight of the bait pulls nylon off, but into the cast the spool has a centrifugal force of its own. Any feathering of the spool by the thumb must be done gently and smoothly. Happily, most spinning multipliers have a brake device linked to the weight of a spinning lure that prevents backlashes. Casts of equal distance can be made with regularity. Stopping a bait is done by clamping down on the turning spool.

Most bad casts come about from a jerky, stunted casting action that pulls line off in an erratic manner. The best way to avoid the dreaded bird's nest is to practise casting until a smooth, easy action is developed. Once learned properly, casting becomes second nature.

The overhead cast (see pages 82–83)

Grip the rod firmly but keep the muscles loose, do not get too tense. Open the reel bale arm (B) after picking up the reel line on your index finger (A). Sight along the extended rod (1) to establish where the bait is intended to land. Bring the rod back smartly to an upright position (2) trying to ensure that it is absolutely perpendicular. The lure will continue to travel beyond your shoulder and you will feel its weight creating a pull at the rod tip. The rod is now in compression. Turn the wrist forward with a flicking motion (3). The spring in the rod blank will transfer the build-up of energy to the lure, which shoots forward. The release position (C) can be fairly critical. If released too early the bait adopts a high trajectory, falling far short of the expected cast distance. Releasing too late again cuts down the distance by flattening the trajectory. Ideally the index finger should be straightened just as the rod and lure have passed beyond the angler's extended arm.

Lower the rod gradually as the lure flies through the air to the planned

OVERHEAD CAST: using a single-handed spinning rod

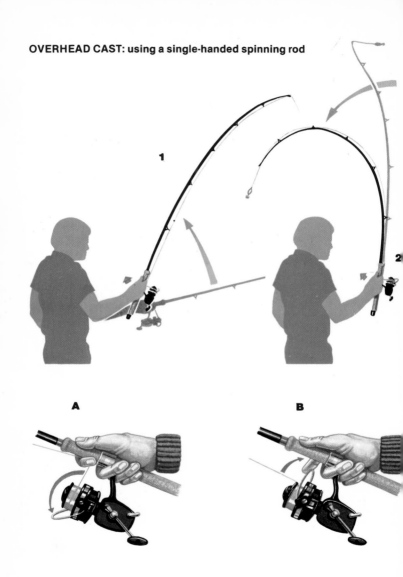

A

B

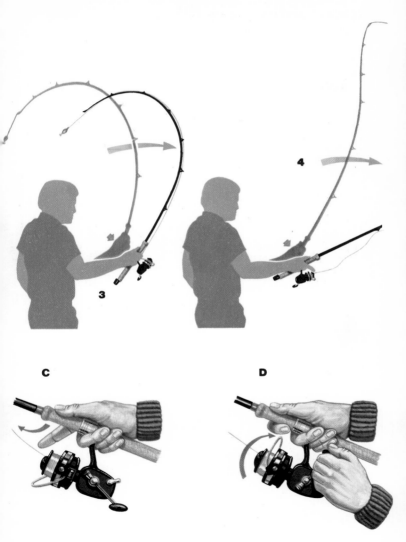

3

4

C

D

SIDE-CAST: with single-handed spinning rod

Rod is swung back across the angler's body

Short trace to aid accuracy of cast and reduce risk of tangling in bushes

CASTING UNDERARM: with a single-handed spinning rod

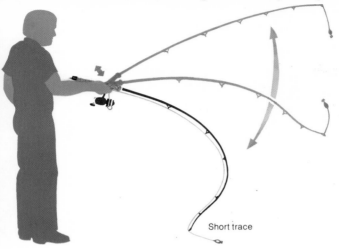

Short trace

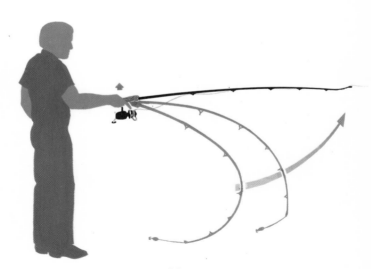

CASTING WITH A DOUBLE-HANDED ROD

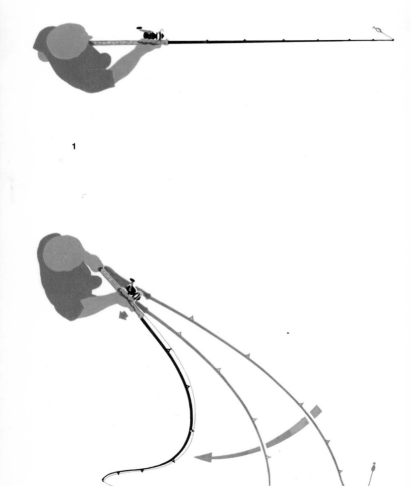

1

2

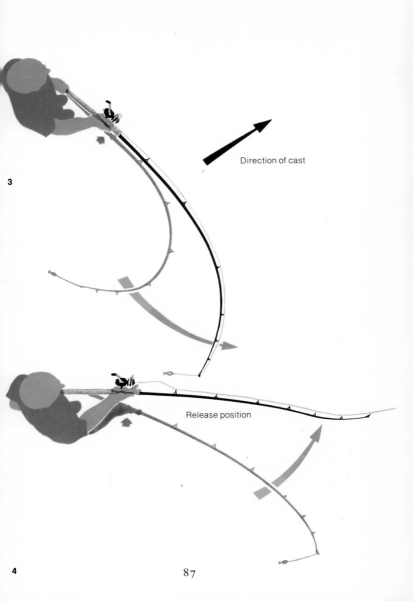

3

Direction of cast

Release position

4

dropping zone. Keep your eyes on its travel so that, if necessary, the flight of the lure can be arrested by dropping the index finger onto the nylon as it runs over the spool rim. Constantly sighting along the rod at each stage of the overhead cast will assist you in making accurate casts, repeatedly placing the bait where you want it to go. As the bait hits the water, close the bale arm by turning the reel handle or flicking the bale arm over, if the reel has that facility. Allow time for the lure to drop down through the water to the depth at which you want it to fish.

From the illustrations it can be seen that the wrist, grip on the handle and position of the thumb are all important to successful single-hand casting. Where possible, adjust the position of the reel to bring the point of rod balance just forward of the casting hand.

The underarm cast (see pages 84–85)

There will be times when an overhead cast is made impossible by the presence of overhanging trees and bushes, which also make a sidecast difficult to execute. This form of cast will put a bait out over shortish distances but it has to be practised as the release position is absolutely critical. The bait must be on a short trace that brings it as near the rod tip as can be achieved. Turn the wrist over so that the back of the hand is uppermost. Attempting the underarm cast with your thumb on top of the rod would be hard to achieve, and possibly you could severely strain something! Flick the rod from a horizontal position down sharply. The bait will swing in towards the angler's knees. As the rod straightens back to the horizonal release the line as the bait flies forward. You will be surprised at the ease with which a reasonable cast can be achieved. Some anglers hold the treble hook in their fingers while pulling the rod into compression. Release of the hook shoots the bait forward like an arrow. It does work well in confined places but there is considerable risk of the angler hooking himself.

Casting with a double-handed rod (see pages 86–87)

The rod is gripped with two fingers either side of the fixed-spool reel. The thumb is not pressed hard against the shoulder of the cork handle. The main task of the right hand and arm is to provide thrust to the rod while the left hand tethers the end of the handle. Stand slightly inclined away from the direction of the cast. Swing the rod back so that the rod is slightly above shoulder height. When a pull from the lure is felt begin to straighten the right arm. Progressively build up the casting power to a punch. At the same time the left hand will pull the handle into the angler's hips.

The bait will speed forward to the release position, which is just before the rod straightens. Follow through with the rod so that it points in the direction of the cast. Control can be exercised over the flying lure should it be heading for a snag. Try to make the forward cast *climb up the hill* by raising the rod as the cast is made, pointing the tip to a 2 o'clock aspect as it passes your shoulder. This upward lift will ensure a correct trajectory; assuming a 3 ft (or about 1 m) length from the rod tip.

Magnificent surroundings – one of the joys of spinning fast water.

FRESHWATER SPINNING SPECIES

Spinning for perch

The perch, *Perca fluviatilis*, is a member of a huge, world-wide family of fishes. Our representative of this family, a gaily striped, hump-backed predator, has become fairly known as the favourite quarry for small boys because, when juvenile, the perch will grab at almost any bait offered. Although as a small fish it takes planktonic animals, the perch soon turns its attention to the fry of other species. The fish is also capable of cannibalism; on those small ponds that have a population wholly composed of perch the older fish exist on a diet of their own kind.

We become interested in the perch as a spinning species when the fish attain weights of 1 lb (0.4 kg) or so. Though primarily a shoalfish in its juvenile years, big perch become solitary in habit. They haunt places which offer them the opportunity for ambush, and we must recognize those situations. In a lake, perch could be widespread but, in terms of their particular territory, they seek underwater obstructions to give them cover. These areas are where trees have fallen into the water or osiers grow, trailing branches below the surface. Undercut banks are another favourite place as well as the shadowed areas created by landing

Left *An angler spinning for perch, at Duddingston Loch, Edinburgh. He looks to be just at the start of the cast. The other angler is a little too near, especially when others are spinning, for a treble can inflict a nasty wound if the cast goes astray and lodges painfully in some part of an angler's unprotected person.* Right *The perch,* Perca fluviatilis. *In the normally murky conditions of most British stillwaters carrying a head of coarse fishes, this handsome fish's stripes would blend well into the background of weeds. From here, the perch will make forays, scattering shoals of foodfish.*

stages. I've caught a number of sizeable perch from beneath moored motor cruisers in Loch Lomond. In short, the perch likes cover and darkness from where it can pounce on likely prey.

In rivers and streams, the ideal perch habitat is little different. The fish will choose the same ambush positions relative to the two factors that govern their choice of a home. Any reed-fringed margin or bank that has piles driven in to retain the soil is worthy of searching out. The fish will avoid the main current flow, preferring to lie just off slacks and eddies formed as the current sweeps around sharp corners or into bays.

Probably the best indication of the presence of feeding perch is the behaviour of the smaller shoalfishes. If you see fry burst from below the surface in clouds it is safe to assume the activity of a predator. Perch will never be far away from the clouds of yearling fry that lie in the shallow margins. But the presence of the hunting fish is hard to detect even with polarised spectacles. Their camouflage is near perfect as they glide in front of reed stems. The fleshy red fins are dulled in water, so one does not get much more than a fleeting glimpse of a bulky shadow lying in wait.

Top right *Fish will use the reed cover of the shallow margins.* **Right** *Perch avoid current pressure, preferring the slack water.* **Below** *Reedbeds form camouflage for perch and pike to strike from.*

TERRITORY IN SMALL LAKE

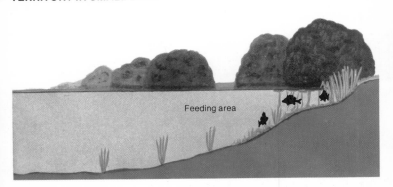

Feeding area

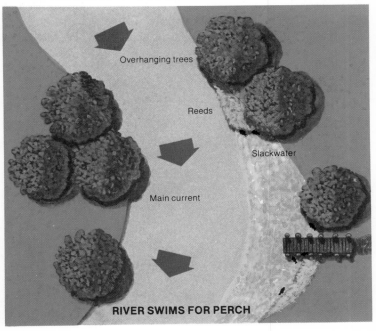

Overhanging trees

Reeds

Slackwater

Main current

RIVER SWIMS FOR PERCH

Left *A bag of sizeable perch.*
Right *Even though this lure is
too big for perch, no doubt the
twirling blade was too exciting
for it to ignore.* Right below *The
visual and vibratory signals of a
blade spinner create an illusion
of a frightened, fleeing fish.*

Because it chases and scatters smaller fish the perch is conditioned to expect the same kind of disturbance in a bait. For this reason the blade spinner appears to be more acceptable than the slower, undulating movement produced by a spoon. The spinner needs to move fast, with plenty of flash and colour. Size of bait is an important factor in successful attraction and hooking. Relative to its body size, the perch's mouth is fairly small which means that we have to choose the bait with care. I find that Nos. 1–3 spinners are about right for all but the huge perch. The treble hook should be as sharp as possible for this fish can come at a bait, hit it hard and yet not get hooked. It should not be due to blunt hooks.

Most blade spinners are given a size. The table establishes their casting weight:

Size	grams
1	1
2	3
3	5
4	7
5	9

The size of the blade spinner is usually related to the size of fish expected, so additional weight may be needed to meet the rod's casting performance. Add weight in the form of a Wye or barrel lead placed uptrace, one of a dulled appearance is preferred as perch will strike at a gleaming lead.

In the river, the blade spinner can be cast across and down the current so that it fishes round in an arc. In slow-running water the bait will have a slow, fluttering motion that is most enticing to perch. Any speed on the river's flow will bring the spinner across-river with the blade twirling fast, giving the illusion of a flashing dace. On many blade spinners the edge of the blade is pressed out with a fluted edge, said to set up fish-like vibrations in the water guaranteed to attract feeding predators.

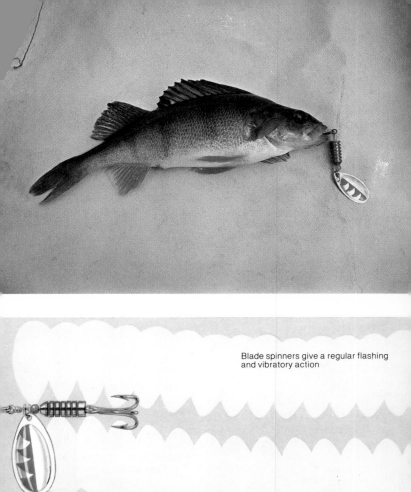

Blade spinners give a regular flashing and vibratory action

In stillwater, try a retrieval system based on winding the spinner back, then letting it sink for a few moments before winding once more. The combination of spinning and sink-and-draw will give fish more time to home in on the bait. When hooked, the perch gives a dashing fight that changes direction with sudden, jerky movements. The fish isn't very powerful and the fight does not become a dour, head-shaking battle – but it's fun! If there is one problem, it is that pike may also take an interest in the spinner. Their teeth would quickly slash through the nylon trace, so many spinfishers use the lightest possible wire trace, about 6 in (15.2 cm) long, in an effort to hold those pike that do grab the spinner. It is usually small pike that attack the fast-moving blade spinner, rather than the larger fish who seek a bigger meal.

Remove hooks from perch with artery forceps. It is usual to find that the fish has only one prong of the treble in its mouth or possibly two. Rarely do they engulf the whole bait. Take care in handling the fish, as the first dorsal fin is spined and can inflict a sharp and painful wound. The fish's gillcases are also armed with sharp, bony plates.

There is one other small lure which works well when spinning on tiny streams for the perch that lie in the deeper water beyond shallows. The devon minnow, particularly useful when trout fishing, gives the illusion of a little fish rapidly swimming across the stream. I've had perch follow the minnow around as it arced across the water, then making its attack as the lure slowed in its spin, coming to the slack under my bank. The metal minnow is best, as it has the necessary casting weight to be flicked across, yet, in the 1 in (25 mm) size, doesn't sink too quickly.

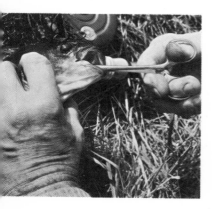

Left *Removing a blade spinner from a perch with the aid of artery forceps.* Right *Only the blue-bodied bait is a true devon minnow. The others are all variations on the same twirling fish-like theme.* Far right *Some drop-minnow rigs, used by French anglers to fish both sink-and-draw and to spin a deadbait. The lead jighead and stiff wire flight can be taken apart to allow a small dead fish to be threaded on. The rig is completed by the addition of a suitably sized hook.*

The devon minnow works best when allowed to swing with the current. It does not seem to have the same attraction when used as a normal cast-and-retrieve bait. It's a lure that can be fluttered in the current. By this, I mean that the speed at which it crosses a stream can be regulated, to some extent, by the way in which it is fished. Try raising and lowering the rod tip, which momentarily halts the bait's progress.

Since perch spend much of their time harrying the shoals of small fry, it follows that they can be caught using the natural fish as a bait. Dead minnows and the smallest roach are ideal lures fished as sink-and-draw attractors. Some lead, to give the deadbait weight for the cast and to get it to sink fairly quickly, is necessary. The French have a simple mount, made up as a stiff wire flight with a leaded jighead, that can be adapted for this purpose. It works well when distance casting is necessary but I'm not certain that the stiffness of the mount helps when perch fishing. Although they will strike, cheekily, at a moving spinner, big perch are sometimes wary of a natural bait that is worked through their territory. I've lost fish that mouthed the bait, found something not to their liking and smartly dropped the offering.

Probably the best baiting system is to liphook a minnow, or similar bait, on a nylon trace with any casting weight added as a single swan shot pinched on to the reel line about 2 ft (0.6 m) above the hook. In earlier times the 'drop minnow', as the technique was called, was fished using a prepared mount that had an elongated lead thrust down into the deadbait's mouth, and two or three treble hooks, on two fine wire lengths, were pressed into the fish's flanks.

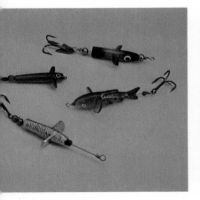 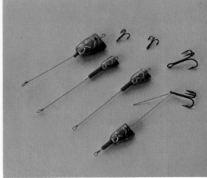

It was a killing method but I still prefer to use just the single hook and lifelike presentation that is achieved by letting the bait flutter down through the water with almost no weight attached to it.

Spinning for pike

Most anglers will have tried spinning for this fish, the largest of our freshwater predators, has a startling reputation. Sometimes hated but also revered, the pike's ferocious appearance and size have created all manner of legends. Without doubt the species does produce extremely large specimens, as Fred Buller found in a detailed research on pike. Many foul deeds are attributed to *Esox lucius*. For certain, the pike takes ducklings, water voles and other surface-swimming animals but it is not the most efficient killer that anglers insist it is. The brown trout must surely rate as the supreme predator. The pike searches out the aged, sickly and dead, whereas the brown trout feeds on the young of every species occupying its habitat.

It is this preference that the pike has for an easy meal that makes it fall to our lures. We spin them in a manner that the pike associates with a fish that is not in full possession of itself, or we put the lure into a position where fit and alert shoalfish never go—but, above all, we hunt the pike, taking the artificials into its own backyard.

Nobody could mistake the pike. It's lean, has a hungry look and eyes, set front-facing, that stare at you. A muscular fish made for fast movement, over short distances. The large tail and dorsal fin, placed far back on the body, give the fish that power and control of direction essential to the expert in ambush. Those eyes, ever watchful, give the pike binocular vision perfect for establishing how far it has to strike—and accuracy is vital if the pike is to be successful.

Like the perch, this species has superb camouflage when hiding among reeds and waterweed. The pike's mottled skin blends perfectly into the light and shadow of its environment.

Pike are said to have a definite feeding cycle with a period of dormant behaviour leading up to a time when they almost go into a feeding frenzy. Whether this cycle is common to all age groups and sexes I do not know, but without doubt pike seem to come on feed quite suddenly. I've had spinning days when nothing moved in the water, then without apparent change in the light or temperature pike after pike chased or struck at the moving bait.

The species is territorial. Even small fish will repeatedly dash out from an established lie to inspect a passing lure. Then they retreat into the same hiding place. I suggest that pike are not solitary in habit until

Far left Our finest predator, the cunning, deadly pike. Right There is something challenging about spinning a reedfilled pond known to hold pike. Accuracy in placing the bait is vital. Far right The pike has binocular vision in the forward plane. It can also detect movement behind it. Therefore a lure spun at the rear of the pike may well trigger off an attacking lunge.

THE PIKE'S BINOCULAR VISION

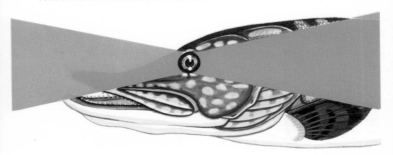

99

PIKE FEEDING CYCLE

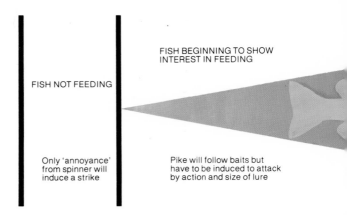

FISH NOT FEEDING

FISH BEGINNING TO SHOW INTEREST IN FEEDING

Only 'annoyance' from spinner will induce a strike

Pike will follow baits but have to be induced to attack by action and size of lure

attaining quite large size. The males never grow much larger than 10 lb (4.5 kg), or so, and may well be the fish that I have often seen lying together in a small stream where it junctions into a big river. Like a pack of submarines, they lie in wait for the downstream migration of salmon smolts. The female pike grow larger and are definitely much slower to attack a spun lure perhaps because their feeding instinct is for a larger mouthful. But offered a largish bait, fished sink-and-draw, and the ladies do become interested.

Pike-holding ground is not too hard to find. These fish have a liking for the slacks that form where a fast current strikes from bank to bank on a winding river. Anything that forms an obstruction to the passage of the current sets up eddies and backwaters and it is here that the species waits. Sunken trees, mudbanks, piling and jetties are places that we all know but it is the less apparent holding ground that we must be able to recognize.

The sudden drop off, where shallow water ends in an underwater cliff, or gully, that only the angler's experience will point out, are perfect pike ground. At spawning time, which is very early in the year, between February and April depending on geographical location, pike move into very shallow areas. Flooded-water meadows and the margins of lakes

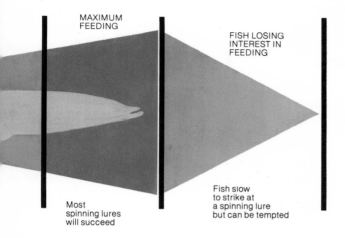

MAXIMUM
FEEDING

FISH LOSING
INTEREST IN
FEEDING

Most
spinning lures
will succeed

Fish slow
to strike at
a spinning lure
but can be tempted

Only observation will tell the angler at what stage in its feeding cycle a known pike has reached. Rarely will a bait or lure presented to a pike when it is in its satiated state result in a take. Its feeding instinct must be aroused and the fish hungry.

and ponds, where winter rain has raised the level, are sought out. The large female fish are joined by a pack of lesser males at this time. It is possible that the two sexes remain apart as soon as the breeding activity is over for the smaller males could be regarded as a potential meal by their much larger consorts.

Having established a pikey area, it must be fished with some system. Allen Edwards suggests three casts to the same position are required. The first cast wakes the pike up, the second gets it 'on the fin' (as Allen would describe it) and the third cast ought to be followed and taken. There is considerable merit in this thinking. Pike don't immediately tear in and grab a lure, but will often follow it right up to the angler's feet, making a close inspection. If the lure is moved fast over the last short distance the pike is sufficiently aware that it tends to hit hard. I think that there are many occasions when we spin over a patch of ground without giving the pike time to react to the sight of a bait. Then off we

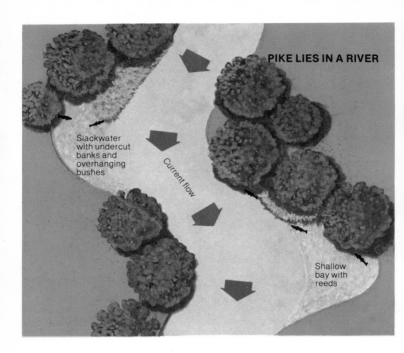

PIKE LIES IN A RIVER

Slackwater with undercut banks and overhanging bushes

Current flow

Shallow bay with reeds

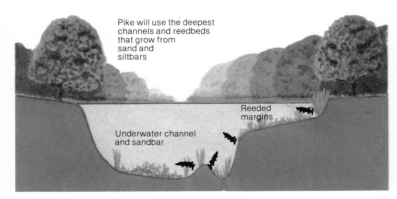

Pike will use the deepest channels and reedbeds that grow from sand and siltbars

Reeded margins

Underwater channel and sandbar

go, assuming that there are no fish in the area. But what we may have done is succeed in awakening an interest in the predator that a following angler may benefit from!

On a slow-moving river or canal one ought to adopt a policy of fan casting, with a spread of consecutive casts that cover a large area. Allen's theory still holds good because fish covered by cast A will still see the bait on repeated casts to either side of that point. Waters of this type need to be fished at differing depths as well. The first cast should be fished through just below the surface; following casts are then given time

Left *Pike will lie in quiet waters where there is cover from which to observe the movements of food fish.* Below *Search the water with the lure to the right and left of the first cast. Then repeat this at varying depths, working steadily along the water's edge.*

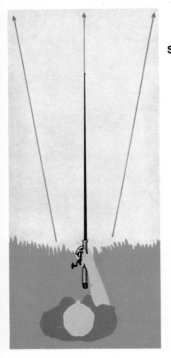

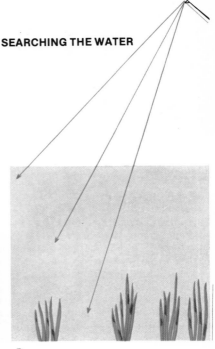

SEARCHING THE WATER

for the bait to drop lower in the water, for it does not always happen that pike lie on the bottom. I've often seen them hanging motionless in mid-water. As predators, pike go to feed where the action is.

Most small pike hit a spinner hard. The angler is left in no doubt as to what has happened. The hooked fish will put up a display of head shaking, with occasional leaps out of the water, especially when held on a taut line. Larger fish may just take the bait and hold it. The line goes solid against the pull of the fish and it is only when the strike is felt that the fish reacts by moving away. Pike seem to make a turn at right angles as soon as they feel resistance to their hold on the lure. The line will be seen to cut away through the surface film.

It is my experience that the larger the pike—and I can only speak of fish up to 25 lb (11.3 kg) as that figure happens to be the heaviest pike that I've had to date—the slower and more dour the fight. I cannot remember having more than about 40 yards (36.5 m) of line out during any fight. Pike do not seem to go far and perhaps this lack of flight distance relates to the fish's territorial behaviour. In common with all fish, pike have no apprehension that they are hooked, only that they have a restraining problem. So, like a small human child, they run to safety.

What happens when a pike is hooked is that it makes small, powerful runs and then lies on the bottom. Whether the fish intends to eject the bait or is 'thinking out its next move' remains a mystery. I've often waited for five minutes or so, letting the line go slightly slack, to get the fish to move. It is no use trying to haul the fish towards you, a line break would surely result. The fish that can be beaten and landed is the fish that moves, because it is expending energy fighting against the sprung curve of the rod.

During the battle, the dangerous period is when the pike comes within a couple of rod lengths of the bank or boat. As soon as the fish sees either, its power to resist becomes doubled. That is the time when a big fish gets its head down and lashes the water with its huge tail. Perhaps it will leap out above the surface although really large specimens rarely do so. The way to handle this sudden activity is to keep the rod high, exerting the full power of the blank against the fish with a line angle that is as near vertical as possible. When that tail lashes from side to side there is always a possibility that the hookhold will give if the line is struck sharply.

Make no sudden movement, just keep the line tight, with a finger on the spool rim as an insurance against a movement that the rod pressure cannot absorb. Tighten line until the fish can be held, lying still, on the surface. Then the net is lowered below the water for the fish to be slid

Above *The Northern pike of Canada has a different coloration from those found in Europe, but it is the same species, its speckled marking being a local variation.* Below *The spoon is designed to simulate the undulating movements of a sick fish.*

SPOON

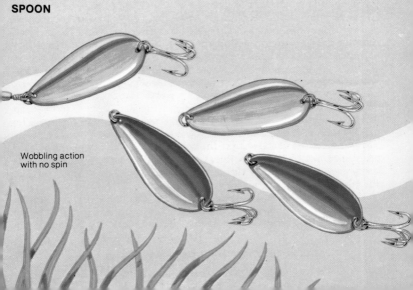

Wobbling action with no spin

across the surface and over the net. A positive lift and all's well!

Whether on a bank of soft grass or in a boat, I do not like to see fish thrashing about. It infers the pike wasn't played out but, more importantly, it is a fish that will suffer unnecessary injury. If possible, get someone to restrain the fish while the job of removing the hooks is completed. To weigh the pike, put it back in the landing net and weigh the lot. One then only has to subtract the weight of the net to arrive at the correct figure. Never weigh a fish by inserting the hook of a spring balance into the fish's gillcase or under the jawbone, the fish could struggle and twist, doing immense harm to itself.

Sometimes a heavy fish puts so much into the fight that it is apparently unconscious and makes no effort to swim when put back into the water. It will recover, but needs help. Hold it upright, with your hands placed either side and under the belly. Gently move the pike backwards and forwards to get water moving over the gills, and within a short time the fish will give a thrust with its tail and be off.

It is possible to land a pike successfully, particularly when fishing from a boat, using only one hand. I'm not suggesting that 30 lb (13.6 kg) fish ought to be boated in this manner, but only the smaller fish up to 10–12 lb (4.5–5.4 kg). The secret in doing this properly is to ensure that

Above *Great care was needed to extract this large copper and red spoon from the pike's throat.* Left *Pike, like most large fish, can be lifted from the water by grasping them firmly behind the gills. But first play them out and draw them into the shallows.*

the pike is ready to be boated. Play it quietly to the boat's side, bringing it to lie alongside the craft. Reach over and place your hand over the pike's back behind the gillcases. Grasp the fish firmly, lifting it in one continuous movement into the boat.

Remove the hooks in the manner described (pages 66–69) keeping hands well away from the recurved teeth with which the species is equipped. If the fish does get hold of you, one's first instinct is to pull the captured hand away. But as you do, those small but incredibly sharp backward-pointing teeth will shred your skin and flesh.

Occasionally a fish will be hooked deep inside the mouth, even at the constriction of the throat. Getting the hook free may well be impossible. Take the wire cutters and cut off the trace wire first. Then try to cut the hook into pieces. With quality cutters, this can be achieved. Pike taken by spinning methods are not often hooked in the throat but if it does happen and the hook cannot be seen, cut the wire as close to the hook

SINK-AND-DRAW

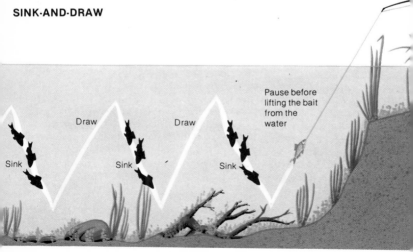

Draw

Draw

Pause before
lifting the bait
from the
water

Sink

Sink

Sink

position as possible. Fish can rid themselves of hooks and some useful research in Holland has shown that pike can live with trebles in the stomach. Fish dissected for research were found to have grown tissue around hooks that were caught in the stomach lining. The fish lived on happily until taken in the nets.

Pike will accept a variety of artificial lures. The small fish are willing to chase fast-spun, smallish baits while the larger pike come more to larger, slow-moving baits and plugs. Fish of all sizes will take lures at some time or other but there are times when the pike refuse to be lured by anything. You will see shoals of small fish swimming past a lying pike with no fear of being attacked. Then, suddenly, the pike comes on feed and the shoalfish scatter. There is no doubt that pike can be induced to feed by fishing an artificial, that annoys rather than suggests food, through their habitat. I've also had times when just a change of lure has been the key to stimulating a feeding phase. In one instance, a change from a mid-water lure to a surface plug was enough to get the pike moving.

Spinning the artificial lure must be an ever-changing, ever-watchful activity on the part of the angler, reacting to what is happening in the water or in the sky above. Lures must be matched to the fish that are being preyed upon, either in colour, shape or the way in which they are worked. A change in the light may well dictate that another colour is demanded. I like to alter the all-over brightness of a bait rather than its colour. A bright bait may well be necessary on a dull day and vice versa but it is the total value of the brightness that is important, not the fact that there is a streak of red paint or yellow spots on the lure.

Most anglers think that the sink-and-draw method of pike fishing does not come within the spinning category. Nonsense! The technique is totally valid, for it sets out to work a bait in a way that induces a strike—and that is spinning at its best. The bait is cast to a position beyond where pike are thought to be lying. After allowing the bait to sink to the desired fishing depth, the rod is lifted to draw the bait up in the water. The bait is then, once again, left to flutter down in the water. At the same time a few turns of the reel are made as the rod tip is lowered. This brings the bait across the river or lake.

Repeat the pattern, bringing the bait towards you until the water has been thoroughly searched. The action can be given additional life by

Top left *After an exciting tussle this youngster successfully nets a good-sized pike from a Nottinghamshire fishery. Note the correct-sized landing net.* Left *The actions of a bait fished sink-and-draw make this method a highly effective spinning technique.*

Above *The wake set up by a surface plug. That and the vibrations it causes simulate a small, swimming animal.* Below *Hooking a pike on the troll while fishing Lough Ree, a huge water that produces large specimens on trolled baits.* Below right *The deep-diving plug's movements reproduce those of a small, ailing fish.*

letting the bait sink and lie on the bottom for a few seconds before continuing with the sink and draw. The object of the technique is to simulate, with a dead fish, the motions of one that is sickly. Pike are the water's scavengers and are constantly watchful for such easy pickings.

Like spinning with the artificial, sink-and-draw is a tiring, ever-moving business that covers a water effectively. It can be practised from the bank or from a boat that is anchored or allowed to drift slowly across the expanse of a stillwater. If the wind is such that the boat is skidding across the water, it is probably best to change to a trolling presentation. This involves drawing the bait, which can be a deadbait or an artificial lure, at a distance behind the boat. Rowing slowly is a superb way in which to troll, with the rod set out from the dinghy at right angles so that any tiny movement of the rod tip is immediately discernible. Because the bait is seen by the pike as something that is moving away from it the take is normally a fairly positive affair.

Pike taken on trolled baits are hooked in the mouth. The fish hasn't the opportunity to grab and turn the bait, so hooking bad enough to call for a surgical operation to remove hooks does not occur. I've always found that the pike are of the small to medium size when caught on a trolled bait. Larry Nixon, from the Pikers of Belfast, assures me that he

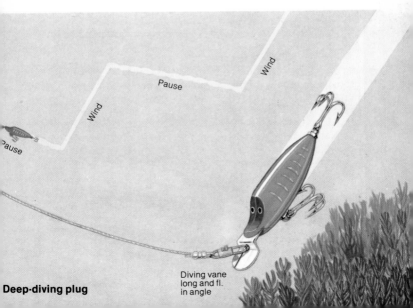

Deep-diving plug

Diving vane
long and fl.
in angle

and the members of his fishing group have taken many fish of 20 lb (9.0 kg) plus, and three of over 30 lb (13.6 kg) on the troll.

I find the use of an echo sounder invaluable when trolling. It does two things; establishes the depth and any changes in it with ample warning so that an alteration in the trolling speed will bring the bait up in the water, and warns of weedbeds or underwater snags. Establishing the position and depth of the weedbeds is vital because, although they can snag the lure, they are also perfect pike habitats. Successful trolling depends on covering fish, not on avoiding the chances of losing a lure.

Trolling, or trailing, a lure can be done from an open bankside. In Holland it is an accepted fishing method where the angler walks the bank pulling a deadbait behind him a short distance from the bank. Obviously the bankside has to be clear of overhanging bushes which will interrupt the troll. But where vegetation prevents a steady troll the angler should fish what can be a pike lie by sink-and-draw before taking up the 'walking troll' beyond the obstruction.

Spinning for zander

In East Anglia, where the zander was an introduction over many years, this species has been marked with the disapproval of many anglers. Originating from Eastern Europe, *Stizostedion lucioperca* has the reputation of a killer of fish that anglers might have enjoyed catching. As an adult fish, the zander does live as a predator on small fish but it is not proven whether its feeding activities or the actions of the people that

Left *Sadly, too many pike have been destroyed by mistaken efforts to improve fisheries. A coarse fishery is not improved by indiscriminate removal of all pike.* **Right** *Clive Loveland, who took the second largest pike on the British record list, nets a smaller one. The record in 1984 stood at 40 lb (18 kg 143 grm), a fish caught by P. Hancock in 1967.* **Below** *Fishing for zander on a Dutch drain in the province of Drente. Since this species' introduction many years ago, zander have now spread throughout the fens and drains of Britain's eastern waters.*

Above *The walleye, a near relative of the zander, is a much-sought-after North American fish.* Below left *The zander,* Stizostedion lucioperca, Below right *A highly experienced angler, Allen Edwards, with a zander caught from a fenland drain.*

manage our waterways have brought about the sorry state of fishing in the fenlands. The species is highly regarded in Continental Europe, where its eating qualities are known and admired.

The zander (also called, wrongly, the pike-perch), is related to the perch family but is not a hybrid between the two fish that give it its popular name. Unlike the pike, zander will thrive in dirty, muddied waters. Its eyesight must be considerably better than the pike which favours clearer streams with less turbidity and pollutants. Spinning for zander is not the leading method of fishing the species in Britain, though European anglers do so on open lakes and clearer waters. Sink-and-draw and livebaiting are regarded as the best methods of attracting the larger fish. In North America, where the zander has a close relative called the walleye, *Stizostedion vitreum*, spinning is a far more widespread technique, accounting for the bulk of catches of all predators.

Fishing fenland drains, where the bulk of zander are found in Britain, has become a matter of presenting deadbaits on legered rigs or livebaiting with small roach and rudd. Coloured water with a moderate run of current suits the leger style. In slower-running streams livebaits can be suspended below small floats, where they are allowed to swim down with the current in a lively fashion. It is in these conditions that the spinner and *worked* deadbait become killing baits.

I know of one particular hotspot for zander in a huge Dutch lake system where a channel, with considerable current, virtually cuts the lake into separate halves. A bed of freshwater mussels is the holding ground for the fish. I am not certain that zander take mussels, it is more likely that bream and rudd feed on the beds and, in turn, are preyed on by the zander. The concentration of fish is heavy and I've seen as many as 20 anglers' dinghies anchored in a confined area. Many of the Dutch fishermen use a paternostered deadbait, casting it from the boat about 30 yards (27.4 m) or so, then working it back in short jerks. They use the lower weight both to aid casting the bait and to set the height above the bottom that the deadbait will be seen by the zander. I much prefer to fish a more conventional, non-tangling rig for a simple sink-and-draw action. The fact that the bait sinks lower onto mud on the lakebed does not matter, provided that the bait can be raised at least 3 ft (91 cm) up in the water on each draw.

Zander seem to be more wary of a bait than pike. For this reason I only use small deadbaits, about 4–6 in (10–15 cm) in length, mounted on a fine-wire snap tackle with two size 8 trebles that are kept sharp. It is important to encourage an immediate strike from the fish. Larger baits seem to get torn off the trace too easily, especially if they are mounted on larger trebles. In my experience most bites are felt as a soft resistance to the draw part of the sink-and-draw action, not a mighty grab. It takes some practice to hit the bite, in fact I have lost contact with many zander that I thought were well hooked. Often, when the terminal rig came back the bait was either lacerated or entirely missing.

Baits should be mounted head towards the angler, on the most flexible wire that can be found. A compromise has to be made between reel line and trace breaking-strain that will give the best fighting chance to a zander while, at the same time, being strong enough to land a pike. Too often a zander bait, correctly presented, attracts the attention of a pike which would easily bite through a nylon trace or prove hard to hold on low breaking strain nylon on the reel. Reel line of 10 lb (4.5 kg) b.s. is a minimum, with wire of 12 lb (5.4 kg) b.s. Particularly when they are big fellows, zander can easily cut wire as it seems to saw across their teeth during the fight. Add any casting weight at least 3 ft (91 cm) from the bait so that the fish is not put off by a complicated rig set-up. A change to a threaded-on bait style, using a single treble emerging from the bait's vent, helps in avoiding the bait being torn off the trace. It also allows the use of a barrel lead as additional casting weight, pushed down into the interior of the bait. The only problem is that mounting the baits takes more time.

Spinning the artificial means using small lures. I prefer the old favourites that incorporate plenty of action. Mepps and Voblex baits are high on my list, followed by the 7–12 gram sizes of Toby and Shanny spoons. The action must not be dependent on speed of retrieve. You cannot zoom a lure through the swim and expect a zander to chase it. These fish are not fast movers. I think they lie above the bottom, holding position until something, that appears edible, happens to move into striking range. The zander is possessed of huge eyes and the fish seems to be able to see a spun lure quite clearly, however murky the water. Add the complication of fishing in the early dawn or late evening, which appear to be the best times for zander fishing and one arrives at the conclusion that zander have remarkably fine eyesight!

Spinning for chub

Most anglers do not, immediately, think of chub as fish that can be caught on spinners. Almost entirely confined to rivers, this species

Above right *In the evening, zander feed round the margins of this Dutch eel trap and often fall to a worked deadbait fished along the side of the curtain of nets.* Right *These lures attract zander when the water is clear, but they have to be fished deep.*

forms a large part of the catches made on baits presented by float or leger during the cold months. But many trout-spinning enthusiasts will tell you of big chub that grabbed their blade spinners—and why not? The chub takes a lot of fry as part of its omnivorous diet.

One should apply perch-fishing tactics when stalking the chub. The larger chub are fond of using similar places to lie up in. Undercut banks and areas of slackish water will harbour one or more of them. Drawing a small lure parallel to the bank of the river covers much of the holding ground associated with this species. The lure can be hung in the water by slowing the rate of retrieve so that the current keeps the blade twirling, which lets the fish see the offering before it moves on.

Although the chub has an inordinately large mouth for its body size, it does not appear to strike at large spinning lures. The tiniest fly spoon or quill minnow is a better type of lure to use. Chub, like trout, spend a large part of the softer months taking floating food, either in the form of surface flies or larvae that fall onto the water. Some of the American popping bugs represent insect larvae and they look very realistic, but I've yet to hook a chub while using them.

Fine line and small lures suit chub spinning admirably but they can cause a problem because winter or summer pike will inhabit the same

Left *The chub,* Leuciscus cephalus. *Of all the members of the carp family, the chub can be the most unpredictable, hard-fighting and exciting fish to be caught on a spun lure.* Right *This tiny lake, high in the mountains of Gran Canaria, holds an introduced population of black bass. They were brought from the mainland and provide excellent sport when fished for with blade spinners worked along the lake's shallow margins. The water is in fact a reservoir, supplying most of the area, the presence of the fish having of course no harmful effect on the purity of the water.*

waters. They will attack the same lures and immediately break the line. Avoiding their intentions is almost impossible, yet attaching the lure to a wire trace will certainly ensure that chub will show little interest. Spinning high in the water does not help as small pike are forced to feed on a catch-as-catch-can basis, competing for food with almost all the other species that the river supports.

Freshwater bass

Introductions of both small-mouth and large-mouth bass from America have been made in European waters in recent years. Both species have been successfully established in many habitats in Spain, France and Germany, coming, originally from North America. The fighting qualities of these fish is such that further introductions have been made, from the now-breeding European stocks, to places such as lakes high in the mountains of the Canary Islands. Both fish have a liking for still or slow-moving waters, where they are sought with spinners and worm baits. Both fish show a resemblance to the perch and their fight is along similar lines.

Freshwater bass live in weedbeds or among the boulders on the bed of rock-strewn lakes. They seem to be extremely territorial in behaviour, never venturing far from their chosen ground. This may well be due to

Left *The large mouth black bass,* Micropterus salmoides, *native to North America.* Below *A Canadian bass habitat.*

the fact that in their normal habitat the fish have many more predatory neighbours than would be found in Europe. Superbly camouflaged, with mottled dark-green colouring and vertical darker stripes, bass are regulators of shoalfish numbers, for they live on a diet of small fry and aquatic animals. They are among the best of freshwater eating fish.

Spinning for trout

The brown trout *Salmo trutta* and rainbow trout *S. gairdneri* are spread or have been introduced throughout Europe. Without doubt they can be regarded as our most important sporting species. Both have a migratory population that travel and spend a large part of their lives feeding in saltwater. The sea trout (also *S. trutta*) adopts a different coloration from the brown trout, having small silver scales with a sprinkling of black dots on the back and flanks. The rainbow trout, which came to us from the west coast of America, has an urge to migrate to the sea and those fish that achieve this are called steelheads.

Brown trout spend their entire life in freshwater, with a slight tolerance towards water that has a small saline content. Unlike the migratory sea trout, they do not pass from the immature parr stage to the smolt, which is the silvery coloured stage that sea trout adopt prior to travelling to the sea. Brown trout never achieve the huge weights that sea

Right *Spinning on one of the innumerable Scottish rivers – the Tyne near Haddington – for wild brown trout.*

trout attain because they do not enjoy the food availability offered by a sojourn in rich coastal waters. But they feed on anything that moves in freshwater, including the fry of other fish and, no doubt, their own parr. Because of this voracious appetite, brown trout have become a sought-after angling species by most fishing methods.

The rainbow trout is generally stocked in stillwaters, although sometimes they are found as escapees from trout farms that border clean rivers. Britain does not have the migratory, steelhead, version of this fish, nor is it found elsewhere in Europe. Rainbow trout are quicker-growing than the brown, feeding on insects and larvae in the wild. The species does not feed to any great extent on live fish, so that they are less likely to take the spun lure. Fly fishing is the best angling technique for the rainbow.

No stream is too small or too high in mountainous country for the brown trout to live in. In the highlands the trout are small, living on a frugal diet of flies, other insects and whatever land invertebrates that get washed into the stream by rain. Fishing for these tiny trout is difficult, because the stream is so small and access to patches of water clear of rocks is not always possible. The small pools that can be found on any highland stream only really offer the opportunity to trundle a worm

down among the stones. Farther downstream, when the weight of water creates a wider and deeper environment, fly, worm and spinning baits are also acceptable offerings to feeding trout.

Trout are never hard to find on a small stream. A few moments spent quietly watching the water will be rewarded by the sight of a fish that rises to the surface, leaving a widening ring as it delicately sucks in the smallest of insects. The fish lie almost motionless behind stones with just a rippling of the body and powerful tail to keep them on station in the current.

As the river gets larger and the current flow greater, colour enters the water as earth and peat leaches into the river. Seeing the trout below the surface becomes harder but their feeding activity remains clear for all to see when the fish burst through the surface film. The spinfisherman stalks his fish by experience of the lies rather than sight of the trout. On the rocky river it is a matter of casting to where trout ought to be, having a mind for the boulders that lurk unseen as a hazard to the lure.

Farther downstream, where the river opens into glides and rippling rapids, the spinner is cast down and across the current to swing round covering the trout lies in a series of arcs. Each time a cast is fished out, the angler takes a pace downstream. I like to fish the spinner carefully

Far left *The brown trout,* Salmo trutta. Left *The sea trout, also* S. trutta. Below *Small blade spinners and spoons for trout.* Right *Two huge male trout from Scotland's Loch Rannoch.*

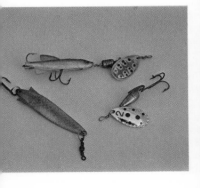

close into the bank as each arc of travel is completed. Many is the fish that can be taken from under the bank, almost below the angler's feet.

Spinning for trout on stillwaters is more difficult in the sense that features that would identify good trout lies are hard to detect. In some of the limestone lakes of Ireland there is little problem in determining the holding ground, where the lake is shallow and rocks and other holding ground is clear to see. The flyfisher covers the water exactly as the spinfisher does when searching water from the bankside, each of them casting to likely spots. When out on the lake their technique divides somewhat. Fly fishing is done with the boat on the drift, letting the wind push the angler towards fish feeding below the surface. The spin-fisherman continues to cast towards holding ground, not hoping to cover fish but seeking them out. The only time one would apply a system based on *happening* onto fish is when trolling a spinning bait!

Trout vary in size and feeding behaviour. In waters where the food availability is good one can expect to find a number of big trout that have grown large feeding on lesser brethren. Their cannibal behaviour results in anglers' tales and different names being given to these fish as though they represented a completely different species. The ferox, of Scotland, has a fantastic reputation for size, ferocity of fight and ugliness, most of which is thoroughly deserved! But it is in fact, like all the other so-called separate trout species, only a huge brown trout.

In Ireland and Scotland a number of lakes are known to hold these huge cannibal fish. Most of those caught have come to large spoons or trolled deadbaits worked at depths not normally associated with trout fishing. Catching the ferox is not an everyday experience and those that hit the angling headlines are taken in one confined period, at the springtime spawning, when they leave the deep water to enter feeder streams and enter the angler's province.

I use small-blade spinners for trout fishing. They have the necessary flash of bright movement to attract the trout. The smaller sizes of popular spoons, providing they have enough action, are also good. What is demanded of both forms of lure is that the treble is of the correct size and the points of the hook sharp.

For many years the devon minnow was the trout angler's standby bait. Made in a variety of sizes and colour patterns, it was a bait with the possibility of many applications. Made of wood, the devon could be fished through at any depth by adjustment of fine weight loading, applied as lead wire wrapped around the wire mount that passes through the body of the minnow. This bait can be fished very slowly, the celluloid vanes giving enough spin in the current to disguise the

Right *A typical stillwater habitat, the vast expanse of Lough Ree, on Ireland's Shannon system. A good head of huge pike predate on the specimen-sized brown trout that share the water.* Below *Christopher Shepley shown getting to grips with one of the Rannoch trout during a session in the brisk air of the early spring sunshine.* Far below *A quill minnow, traditionally in swan or goose quill for spinning for salmon and trout.*

QUILL MINNOW

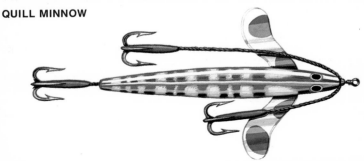

artificialness of the lure. The only point I would make about devons is that the action is too regular. I have a feeling for lures that behave erratically, but whether trout share that opinion, I'll never know!

From America we have a whole army of new lures for spinning and trolling. Many of them are aimed at the trout family, with special application for very deep lakes or to urge an attack based on the suggestion that another fish was already chasing the lure. I've used them in Canada and they worked. Perhaps we ought to give them a try before dismissing them all as gaudy imports!

Spinning with the blade spinner or the devon minnow sets up a lot of line twist, so the trace make-up is important. A nylon trace of 3 ft (91 cm) using one swivel at the lure and another to join the reel line, is necessary. The addition of an anti-kink vane or weight helps a lot. Keep the swivel sizes small and ensure that they do turn. Trout are among the most suspicious of fish, so keep the rigs simple and unencumbered.

When I was a boy there was a method of trout fishing, loosely based on sink-and-draw, using a live minnow. It was used extensively on the Thames for the large trout that favour the weirpools, and the drop-minnow, as it was called, accounted for a lot of fish. Recently I had occasion to visit a river on which there was a millpool. Though disused, the current was held back somewhat by a broken dam and hatches. A very big trout was known to lie just out of the current as it poured down the wheel sluice. Naturally, I had a go for the fish and succeeded in partially hooking it on a tiny roach, but the trout tore the bait from the single hook as though it had never fed before! Nothing would encourage it to strike again, yet I wonder if that old historical technique of drop-minnow might not have more uses than were realised in the past. •

The problem of spinning or working a fish bait for trout is that much of the game fishing legislation prevents us using other than fly-fishing methods. I suppose the inference is that spinning catches too many fish or is too easy. Not so! It is only another way to fish that ought to be recognised as totally legitimate in the same way that stripping huge lures on sunk lines is regarded as legitimate fly fishing! Before you attempt to spin any water for trout, make sure that the technique is allowed.

Spinning on salmon rivers

Saloon-bar discussions suggest that fly fishing is the only satisfactory way in which to catch a salmon. There may be some truth in that when the talk goes on to the fish's environment and the way in which the angler sees so much of the fish and their taking methods. But, there are times and situations where the spinner is needed if anything is to be caught. Salmon are not selective about baits and lures. They do not move to the attack on the basis that they need food. The fish are either protecting a favoured lie or they are 'annoyed'!

Obviously salmon will, at different times, move to a fly or artificial lure on the basis of its colour, size or motion. But they are not bent on

Top right *The River Tay, one of Scotland's most important salmon rivers. The angler, almost hidden from view below the rock bluff projecting from the left, spins into the streamy, riffled water as it opens out into a deeper, inviting pool likely to be the resting place of a salmon.* **Right** *The salmon, Salmo salar. Why it falls to spinner and fly when in theory it should not feed in freshwater is still an unsolved problem and an abiding topic when game fishermen meet. That the majestic salmon is drawn to strike at such lures accounts for some of the most rewarding and exciting battles between angler and fish.*

eating it. Something, which can be an instinct from earlier times spent feeding in the sea, or a pure reflex action that urges the fish to chase away the bait that intrudes into the salmon's temporary territory, is the key to its predatory behaviour. But the problem is so far unsolved.

As if that is not enough, factors of temperature, water colour and height of the stream all play a part in the way in which the salmon behaves and affect the choice that the salmon angler makes when trying on his lure. It is often said that the only successful salmon fisher is one who lives by the waterside. Very true, but meant in two ways. To live close to fishing means that one can react immediately to changes in the condition of the river, but it also means that more time can be spent reading every possible permutation of factors that affect fish behaviour.

Salmon are *unique* in choosing and using particular resting places, or lies, year after year. The position of the lies depends on the three factors mentioned earlier—temperature, water colour, depth—though there may be subtle changes depending on the needs of fish. What we have to do is meet those requirements by presenting a suitable bait at a moment in time that coincides with a taking period. Fish stationed in a resting place are the fish likely to move to the bait. Travelling salmon, those that are on passage from the sea up to the headwaters, are rarely interested in

Left *One of Norway's finest salmon rivers, the Driva, enjoys big runs of salmon and sea trout.* Below *A fine spring salmon caught by Barrie Welham while fishing the Dee at Barlogie, Scotland.*

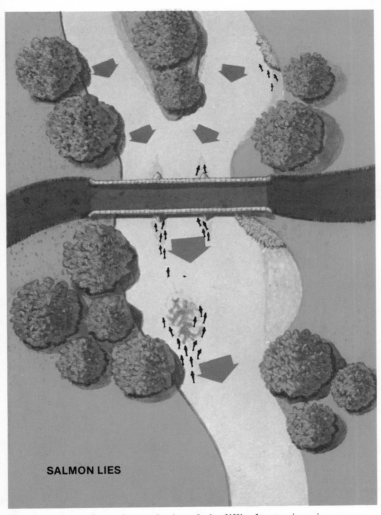

SALMON LIES

Resting places for salmon during their difficult up-river journeys.

taking a lure although they may pause in the journey at places that present an obstacle to their upstream movement. Weirs, strong rapids and salmon ladders are all spots where salmon will stop for a while, perhaps to rest before attempting to overcome the obstacle.

Spinning methods differ throughout the season. In the heavy water of the early spring, fish will be lying just outside the edge of the streamy water. They avoid the main force of current, preferring the comfort of a steady flow that provides oxygen without too much effort on the part of the fish, to maintain its position. I like to get the bait down to fish about 1 ft (30 cm) above the riverbed. The pace of current will dictate the size and weight of lure, although the speed at which it swings across the river can be controlled by judicious use of the rod. Keeping the tip fairly high swings the bait around and cushions any vigorous takes. Lowering the tip, when a particular area is being covered, will halt the speed momentarily but beware of pointing the rod and line directly at the fish. It could result in a breakage if a salmon takes and turns sharply with the full flow adding its power to the speed of the moving fish.

The pace-downstream-per-cast system is the best to ensure that the water has been truly covered. If a fish moves, remain at the same place,

It is important to cover all the water when spinning otherwise likely fish may be missed. At each cast, try to create a pattern of steps, taking one pace upstream when the lure has been retrieved.

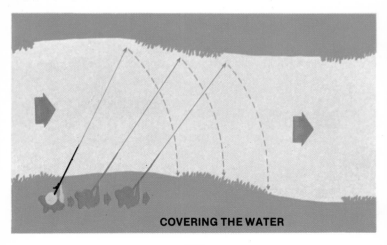

COVERING THE WATER

Salmon spoons: Three Shanny spoons (top); an American lure, Seadevlet (centre); Diawa Attackers, with a reflecting surface (right); and the largest of the Shanny lure series (bottom).

shortening the cast a trifle so that the fish sees the bait swing around ahead of it. Unfortunately, with the heavy water of spring, so much of what is happening is invisible to the angler. In deep glides and pools the action is more often felt rather than seen. Everyone likes to see salmon, even if they are slow to take. But noisy splashing activity is usually the sign of kelts in the pool.

On any salmon river there are running lies, places where fish that have just arrived, or are on passage to the spawning redds, pause for a short time to rest. Knowing where these lies are and the definite path between each of them is the knowledge of the gillie. This man, found in association with all salmon fisheries, spends his life on the river teaching, explaining and providing the active assistance that most people need when they experience the heart-stopping take of a good fish.

Salmon run the river on a route which may meander across the width of the stream. Obviously a lure that is swinging across the river's breadth covers the path and any lies on it for but a brief moment. The expert knowledge of a gillie will aid any angler in presenting his bait exactly where it should be, cutting down on wasted time fishing water that never will hold a fish.

I use the longest of my spinning rods for salmon fishing. The best of them, a 10 ft (3 m) fibreglass rod with a medium action, suits the rhythm of continuous casting where any easy, measured cast is vital. My choice of reel is between a multiplier, loaded with nylon of 15–18 lb (6.8–8.1 kg) b.s. and a skirted, fixed-spool reel that holds enough 12 lb (5.4 kg) nylon to cope with the fight of a salmon on smaller rivers. I confess that the multiplier does most of the work.

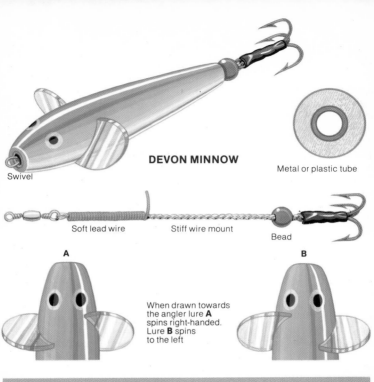

DEVON MINNOW

Swivel

Metal or plastic tube

Soft lead wire   Stiff wire mount   Bead

A   **B**

When drawn towards
the angler lure **A**
spins right-handed.
Lure **B** spins
to the left

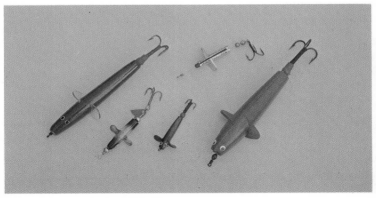

In spring the baits are wobbling spoons. There are hundreds of patterns to choose from, yet I seem to lean heavily on just two types: the Toby and Shanny. Both have a gentle, undulating motion and cast well against strong winds. When the water warms up a little the devons come into play. All are made of wood so that they fish in mid-water, although the addition of some soft lead wire takes them down to the riverbed. The devon has a regular spinning action, but it can be hung in a current without nosediving like a metal spoon. I do not like using plugs on a salmon river. They have too much action when a strong current takes hold. Fish get hooked outside the mouth and the multiple hooks tend to foul in the river bottom. Salmon fishing involves long casting and plugs have a nasty habit of turning in the wind and getting the trace wrapped up in the hooks. Their place is in stillwater fishing or on rivers with a slow, steady current.

Long casting with light lures requires the addition of some weight. This is best added as a Wye, or possibly Jardine spiral lead, above the ball-bearing swivel that joins trace to reel line. Devons will often need added weight as casting them on heavy nylon is difficult. Do not add weight above a metal lure as the two chunks of metal will cartwheel through the air, getting tangled along the way.

Top left *The parts of a carved, wooden minnow. The fins can be adjusted to give either right or left-handed spin. This is a very versatile lure.* **Left** *Metal, plastic and traditional wooden devons for salmon spinning.* **Below** *A male salmon in its spawning habit, showing the characteristic hooked lower jaw, called the kype.* **Right** *Four superb freshrun salmon from Scotland's River Tay.*

Above *Lough Currane, Co. Kerry, is unique in having salmon, sea trout and brown trout fishing of the highest quality. The lough is only a short distance from the Atlantic Ocean.* Below left *Tailing a salmon caught from the River Tweed, near Peebles. The noose cannot slip from the tail.* Below right *The char,* Salvelinus alpinus.

The middle of the year gives us lower water and a temperature that encourages salmon to rise to a bait. Smaller devons and blade spinners fish well just under the surface and moving fish can be detected with some certainty. Summer fish move into the river. These delicate salmon, known as grilse, weigh only 5 lb (2.2 kg) or so and are fish that have spent only one year feeding in saltwater. They are sprightly and give flashing sport on the correct balanced tackle. If legislation allows spinning at this time of year, reducing the tackle strength can be a problem in that there will still be many larger salmon in the middle stretches of most salmon rivers that could wreak havoc with the gear. Fortunately, most springers will have long since departed for the redds.

Playing a salmon

The take of a salmon may be registered in a number of ways: the bait might appear to be hung up, its travel across the river arrested or a savage jerk may herald the take. Generally the fish will make a pretty good job of hooking itself. Steady pressure must then be applied, with the slipping clutch carefully pre-adjusted to give you confidence and the fish something to smooth out its more violent moments. Keep the rod up with the arc of the blank absorbing the power of the fish. Play it cool, keeping the fish on the move. Never let it lie quietly, for then is when it recovers strength while you lose muscle control and patience! Pump the rod in easy, smooth fashion, retrieving line back onto the reel. Make a decision about where you are going to land the fish. This can either be done by beaching it on a flat shore or using a large net.

I like to do the job myself, rather than seek the assistance of somebody eager to help but not necessarily competent. With the rod held high and a controlling finger or thumb on the spool, lead the fish upstream a little so that it is above your position. Lean over and grasp the tail wrist firmly or let the salmon drift back into the open gape of the net. Either system must be done positively and without undue haste. When netting a fish, I slide the handle through my grasp until the net frame can be held. Then it is a simple matter of carrying the fish well away from the water's edge before attempting to inspect the catch. Salmon should be despatched quickly, and humanely, with a sharp blow across the back of the neck at the gillcase joining. A suitable priest can be made by whipping an 8 oz (227 g) casting sea lead onto a short wooden handle. This will give the weight to kill your fish properly.

Spinning for char

In a few mountain lakes in Britain and Ireland, and in the rivers of Arctic regions, we find another member of the salmon family, the char. This remnant of the Ice Age fauna has become landlocked in waters of the

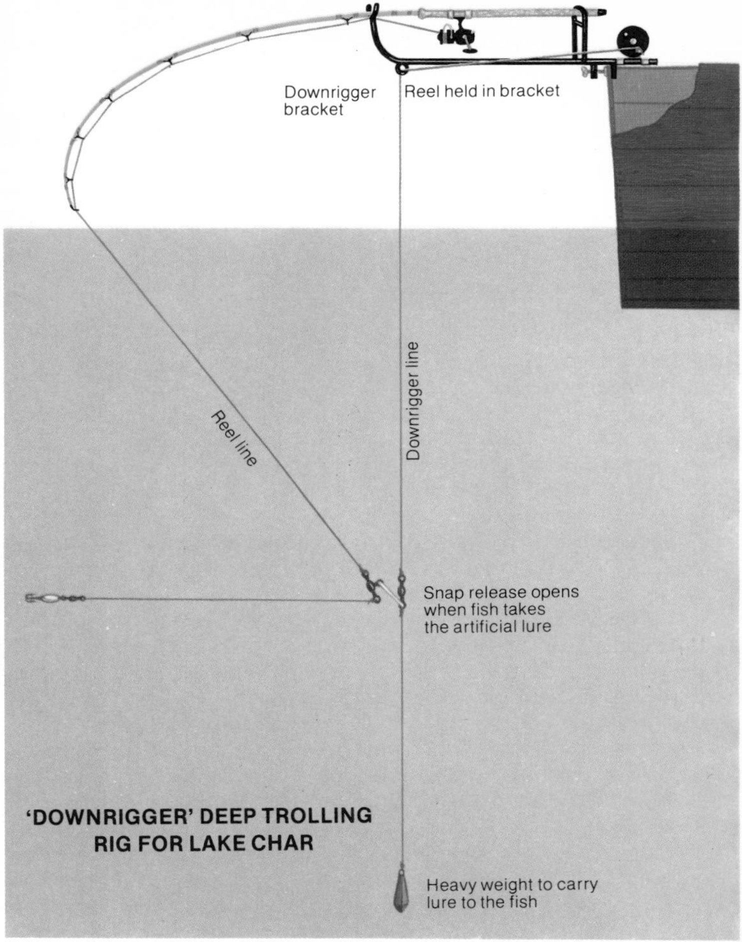

Centrepin reel feeds off line to take lure to feeding depth

Downrigger bracket

Reel held in bracket

Downrigger line

Reel line

Snap release opens when fish takes the artificial lure

'DOWNRIGGER' DEEP TROLLING RIG FOR LAKE CHAR

Heavy weight to carry lure to the fish

British Isles, though in more northerly parts of the world it behaves just like the seatrout. Spawning in freshwater, the char spends most of its life feeding in the sea. Our char, *Salvelinus alpinus*, is found in deep, cold waters where the restrictions of food availability prevent fish from attaining the sizes of char which have the richness of sea plankton to promote their growth.

In Greenland, where I have had superb char fishing, the fish arrive in sea fiords at the end of August. They enter the tiny streams, fed by the many glaciers, to breed. Both spinning and fly techniques are used with no real advantage in either in terms of the size of catch or individual fish. Trout spinning tackle is used, with small-blade spinners and spoons accounting for very big specimens. The bigger lures do not work so well, which must be related to the char's diet of minute crustacea and invertebrates.

In Britain, anglers who fish for the char have to do so with deep-trolled rigs suspended on downriggers, not a very satisfactory way to hook such small fish but necessary when trying for a species that inhabits the deepest water. What is evident is the skill of the professional fishermen of lakes such as Windermere, who troll at depths of 60–80 ft (18.2–24.3 m) with lures of their own making. But eating this fish makes all the effort worthwhile, as the char is noted for its delicate red flesh of superb flavour. Cooked beside an Arctic fiord, nothing could taste better than the char.

Left *Rig for arctic char*. Above *Char habitat in Greenland*. Top right *Char taken on a small blade spinner in tumbling rapids*. Right *One of the pleasures of wilderness angling: anglers about to savour the superlative aroma and taste of waterside-cooked char*.

SPINNING IN THE SEA

The environment for success

Most sea anglers would regard spinning as something to be done when fishing by conventional tactics is unproductive. But spinning at sea should be thought of as a highly skilled method that calls for a degree of knowledge about the spinning species, where they feed and the seasons when annual migration brings them within casting range. The rocky coasts offer the best spinning because the fish have a better food possibility closer in to the shore. Deeper water is less affected by tidal rise and fall, so fishing can be extended throughout the phase. Spinning starts in late spring with the arrival of the migratory fish. Their migration is not necessarily from distant climates, it is more often from very deep water offshore into where the new season promotes a lush growth of feed.

The equipment for saltwater spinning need not differ from that used by freshwater anglers. Rods that will handle pike and salmon are absolutely right for pollack and bass, though the fight has tide action as an added power to the struggle. The 10 ft (3 m), fibreglass rod with a reel loaded with 8–14 lb (3.6–6.3 kg) b.s. nylon suffices. Long casting may be vital to get to fish that swim just outside the inshore spoil, where waves thrash and turn on themselves. Here, the double-handed rod gives a pleasant casting action that is far less tiring through the day's sport.

Spinning for pollack

Although inshore pollack will feed right through any day, I like to think of them as an evening fish. As the light fades and sunlight leaves the water they display a vertical migration, coming up to feed on small fry in the surface film. The pollack chooses to inhabit the rock strewn coasts where its dark-green colouring blends well into the kelps and weed that abound. There is a whole mass of food around and the plankton-bearing currents cling to the coast. On the south and western shores, where the sea is generally much warmer, plankton thickens the water like soup and millions of immature fish feed among it. Pollack move up into the plankton layer, striking at anything edible.

The artificial baits needed should have some resemblance, either in shape or action, and preferably both, to the live creature. Sandeels have a high priority on the diet of pollack and bass and great efforts have been

Rocky shelves, although primarily a shorecasting situation, provide unequalled spinning possibilities. Take care when clambering over wet rocks and watch out for that dangerous, large rogue wave.

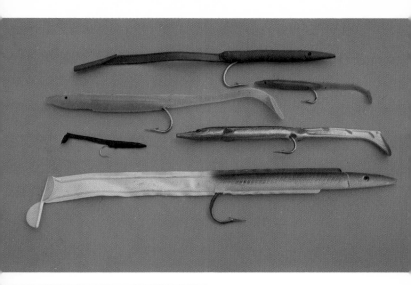

Above *All these lures are quite different forms of artificial sandeel. They can be used to spin shore marks, rock gullies and close-in deep water, for roving pollack and bass.* Left *Pollack, Pollachius pollachius, are powerful, deep-diving reef fish. They haunt rock gullies at high tide in search of small fish and food items dislodged from the cover of the rocks. The largest pollack, those weighing over 20 lb (9 kg) are found round pinnacle reefs in deep water and are the specimens that provide grand sport for the boat angler.* Right *A typical trace for seashore and boat fishing.*

made by many manufacturers to simulate the action of the eel. Some of the artificial eels work well, with tails that wave in the slightest current, but others are more suited to sink-and-draw methods when fished at depth on the offshore wrecks.

Casting sandeels requires additional weight added well above the eel. Placed too close, the weight tends to dampen the eel's trembling action. A barrel lead or spiral should be attached above the connecting trace swivel. Look at the hook that the eel is provided with. Some makers pay little attention to fitting the correct hook and ensuring that it has a sharp point. All they seem to be interested in is that the hook should be large, and often far too large! On a 7 in (17.7 cm) eel the hook needs to be about 6/o size to hook well. Pollack live among weed and I like to have a number of eels fitted with a weedless hook so that I can follow the fish by casting over weeds and kelp. A simple way to give some weedless protection is to bind a length of stiff Alasticum wire, bending the wire to the shape shown. This will help in keeping the point out of weed fronds. Inevitably some lures will get well hung up, but at least fishing in a hazardous situation will cover more fish.

Spoons of silver coloration are also useful, particularly those slim in shape that look like a sandeel swimming. The German sprat is an old

SPINNING TRACE FOR BOAT AND SHORE FISHING

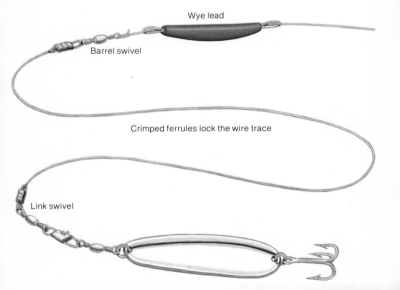

Wye lead

Barrel swivel

Crimped ferrules lock the wire trace

Link swivel

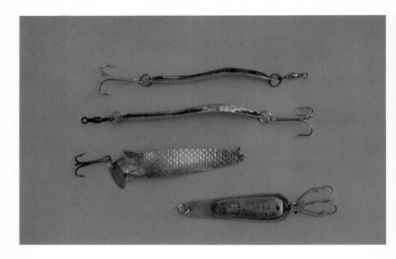

Spoons for sea spinning: Two German sprats (top); Toby (centre); and an Elbe Torsk with added weight for casting, total 49 gr.

favourite that accounts for a lot of fish taken spinning in Ireland. Colour on spoons and eels has little importance when one considers the depths at which lures are spun in the sea. Only 6 ft (1.8 m) down, most colours disappear in muddied waters. Only blue light penetrates the murk and in really clear water even red light disappears within a few fathoms. Lures that are white or blue show up well, red appears black.

Lures can either appear as bright objects or as silhouetted shapes. A dark lure is best used just under the surface where fish lying below it will clearly detect the movement and shape. Farther down, a lure should be lighter, taking on the colour pattern of live fish, which is light below and dark above. Fish that live on reefs and open rocky ground have perfect camouflage suited to the environment and the height in the water at which they swim.

We look for pollack on the top of pinnacle reefs or within the waving weeds on open ground. These fish do venture away from the rocks but never so far that they cannot make a sudden dive to get back to security.

Spinning is a matter of drawing the pollack away from their resting places. These fish are fast and tough, so a lure that is dangled among the rocks will finish tight into them! The hooked pollack has to be held for

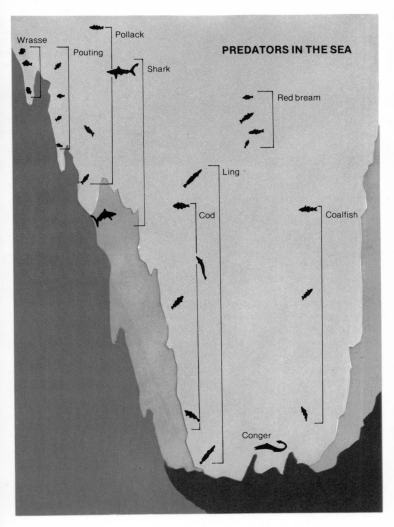

PREDATORS IN THE SEA

Wrasse

Pouting

Pollack

Shark

Red bream

Ling

Cod

Coalfish

Conger

Feeding and security dictate where each species of fish can be found.

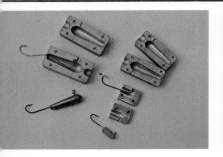

Standard beachcasting lead moulds can be adapted to take an elongated hook link. The eye, for attachment, juts out at right-angles.

A hole and slot have been bored into the mould to enable the eye of the jighead to protrude from the body of the beachcasting weight.

the first moments of the fight with its headlong rush absorbed by the rod. Keep the rod tip high and hope that the fish's head is similarly positioned. Almost all pollack will turn to dive. From the shore it is difficult to prevent fish from getting their heads down but the rod high stance, with an element of side strain to turn the hooked fish, often gives those few moments of control when the fish is strongest.

Ideally, one would fish a reef from a boat, casting lures towards the reef so that the fight is leading the fish away into clear water. One situation that brings ideal spinning possibilities is where there are peninsulas of rock jutting out into the sea, with clear sandy patches between them. If close enough, a cast can be made from one spur towards the rough ground of the next.

Each of these Mr Twister lures has a heavy jighead to assist casting. They are in 1½, 4 and 6 oz (42, 113 and 170 gr) sizes. The heads can be painted or left in natural finish. This seems to make no difference to their fish-catching properties.

The dangerous part of making lead weight at home. The lead is poured with the mould firmly clamped – NOT HAND-HELD – in a bench vice. Take great care!

When it leaves the mould, waste lead at the head of the weight has to be trimmed off. The length of hook should be equal for all lead sizes.

Shallow rocky ground offers the opportunity to troll an artificial eel. Some of the finest sea trolling that I have ever experienced took place while fishing out from Kilmore Quay, in County Wexford. Shallow reefs, extending from the land towards the Saltee Islands, held massive pollack that came to the rubber eels fished only 30 yards (27.4 m) behind a slowly moving boat. Oddly enough, the same area provided the best of bass trolling for years. The Splaugh rock, an area of reef and weed lying out from Rosslare, had a tremendous concentration of bass which were always patrolling the open ground around the rocks. German sprats were the supreme lure, with fish coming to them weighing 8 lb (3.6 kg) and more. Unfortunately, as always happens, the fishing was abused with enormous catches taken by anglers and commercial fishermen. Nowadays it would be difficult to find a comparable meeting place of pollack and bass.

In the sea long-distance casting and sink-and-draw styles demand a heavy lure. The immediate problem is finding lures that work well as they must. I find that the answer is to combine a lure that works well with the necessary casting weight attached. Mr Twisters have caught a lot of pollack for me in both spinning-trolling and sink-and-draw fishing. The lure is sold weightless, although the Americans do supply a small jighead for freshwater baitcasting. I cast a lead jighead in 2, 3 and

5 oz (56, 85, 142 g) sizes that incorporates the correct pattern and length of hook. The Twisters are simply threaded onto the hook, no matter what size of weight is called for.

Spinning for bass

This most prized of coastal fishes can be taken in two defined envionments; estuaries and from the rocky shore. On the open strand, traditionally the bass fisher's hunting ground, the water is too shallow for baits to work well if at all. Our American counterparts cast lures to bass in the surf. Striper fishing is done with big jigs and plugs, but they have more powerful, higher surf and a fish that is eager to hit such lures.

The estuary gives the opportunity of fishing across the current flow on both the making and ebbing tides. Bass are foragers, some anglers might even say scavengers, that work into the river mouths to feed on fry, worms and small crabs. They keep more to the channels than the other well-known forager, the mullet. I make this point for the reason that many times I have been told of massive shoals of bass in the estuary, only to find that they were mullet, splashing and showing their dorsals as they searched the open mudflats. The artificial sandeel is a good lure when fishing the esturial channels. It can be fished with little added weight to hang on the current, with the tail rippling enticingly.

Left *the bass,* Dicentrachus labrax. Below *Bass are a highly prized species for spinning and beachcasting. They haunt the open storm beaches and rock-strewn ground where food is abundant.* Right *An ideal spinning area is the mouth of an inlet or estuary, where the hungry bass follow the incoming tide, snapping at shoals of fry feeding on the mudflats.*

Bass favour lures that have plenty of action and movement. They themselves are fast-moving fish that can hit a spun bait with some force. When using metal lures, such as silver spoons, I fish them fast. Sometimes breaking the surface film just as the live fish do in their attempts to flee from marauding bass. The larger-specimen fish are slower in their activities, they could be said to be scavengers as they lurk around the piers and pilings. A plug of the floating variety, which dives when retrieved can be fished into the dark shadowed places that provide the fish with ambush possibilities. Plugs need very little winding in to get them to work well; the spoons, being heavy, have to be kept on the move to achieve a lifelike presentation. Jerky movements, when the plug is on the surface, can incite an attack response from bass with the chance that harbour pollack will also take an interest.

Fish both tides through on the estuary, for the fish must make a return trip. Although they can tolerate some degree of freshwater, bass drop back on the ebb to resume feeding in the sea proper. They are fish to be stalked. Sometimes, feeding bass can be detected by sudden swirls, accompanied by the sight of fins out of the water, but mostly their arrival is recognised by a frantic escape response by smaller fry. As the fish move, so must you. Bass cover a lot of ground in any feeding situation so

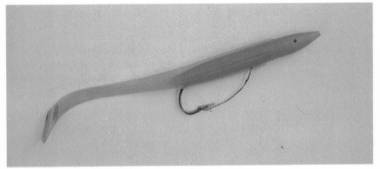

Top *An ideal spinning area, with rocks jutting into the sea onto a clean sandy bottom.* Above *Make an artificial sandeel weedless by attaching a stiff wire shroud to guard the point.* Left *Pollack are caught by spinning from a boat set to drift over pinnacle reefs and rock ledges.* Top right *Bass will feed in a making tide over a sandy beach where there is a surf. The fish follow breakers right to the shore as they forage.*

they have to be followed. The spinfisher has nothing with which to hold fish, his object is in placing lures ahead of the fish to simulate the activities of possible food.

Bass are held off cliff faces and around the rocky ledges by the available food. They feed throughout the tidal phase because the power of maximum tide strength is a dangerous time for small creatures. They are swept out of their hiding places, into the open mouths of the patrolling bass. The fish do not stay still in the water, they are constantly on the move, backwards and forwards, on the alert. This behaviour suits the angler because it means that his artificial lures are not seen constantly above the fish. Familiarity does not set in and a fish that inspects, but rejects a lure, may well hit it on another pass.

Bass do not hide in rocks and weeded areas. They are creatures of the open sea, constantly moving along the face of rock ledges which means that our spinners can be cast to work along the same ground. Occasional hang-ups are impossible to avoid as the weed fronds sweep about in the tide. Weedless hooks can help a lot, especially in areas liberally coated with the soft, brown seaweeds, where they pull through quite easily. Kelp is another story. Thicker than a man's wrist and leathery, very few baits caught up in *Laminaria* ever come back.

If there is one bass habitat that I always try to fish, it is the rock margins that one finds at each end of most bass surf beaches. The rocks are turning points for the bass after each swimming pass along the length of the turning surf. The rocks can be very productive even though fish are spending their time patrolling the breakers. Food tends to be swept along the strand by the lateral currents, finding its way, in concentration, to the margins where the bass spinner lurks.

The sandeel is probably the best lure for this situation, representing something that bass may have passed over while on routine beach patrol. Other small fish, such as gobies, blennies and small rocklings inhabit the rocks, so bass are conditioned to finding fish on what is basically a worm-fishing pitch.

Trolling can play a useful part in bass fishing. The lure, either an artificial or mounted deadbait, is trailed behind a rowboat or slowly-moving powerboat in areas of quiet water, places where bass come in to search. Large harbours and saltwater inlets are ideal, as are deepwater estuaries of rivers found in the western Atlantic waters. The lure, with very little added weight, is moved slowly through the water with the boat performing a zigzag pattern that alternately raises and lowers the offering in the water. If the rod is extended at right angles to the boat's side, a clear indication of a bite is seen as the tip is pulled around against the forward motion of the fishing craft. I've never found the fish put off by the sound and vibration of the engine or noise made as anglers shuffle their feet. If anything, the engine noise served to arouse the interest of the bass.

The fight of a bass is best described as strong and protracted when taken on a spinner. The tethering lead weight of the baitcasting shore

Left *The mackerel,* Scomber scombrus. Below *Spinners for mackerel fishing. The author prefers blade spinners rather than the traditional trolling kinds that need added weight for them to be cast out any distance.* Right *A catch of superb mackerel of $1\frac{1}{2}$-2 lb (0.74-0.9 kg).*

angler prevents bass from showing their true fight. Keep the rod up, as the fight has a series of sudden changes of direction and a landing net of appropriate size is a must!

Mackerel—king of speed

This is a sea fish worthy of any spinfisher's attention. Taken in hundreds by boat anglers as bait, the heavy gear of feathering does nothing for the mackerel's reputation as a fighter. A member of the tunny tribe, mackerel are among the fastest swimmers in the sea and offer delightful sport *on the right gear*. The baitcasting or single-handed rod, balanced to lines of about 5 lb (2.2 kg) or close to, bring the fight into perspective.

Traditional lures, like the so-called mackerel spinner, are intended for trailing behind a moving boat and are far too large. Presentation is always in conjunction with a heavy trolling lead that completely dampens the mackerel's frantic fight. This species should be fished by spinning methods, never on the troll. Ideally, one seeks the fish from early summer to the middle of autumn. The shoals rise to the surface to harry small fry. Detecting feeding mackerel depends very much on the angler's eyesight or, better still, on the ability of our sea birds to find the surface shoals. When the birds are working over a mackerel shoal they can be seen for miles. Gulls, kittiwakes and gannets circle above the fish,

Above *A light spinning rod in action off the Isle of Arran, in the Firth of Clyde, Scotland.*
Left *The garfish,* Belone belone.
Below *The smallest artificial sandeels and tiny blade spinners are the best lures when spinning for garfish. Only the minimum of weight should be added to the trace to provide the best sport. Don't be put off by their green bones when cooked!*

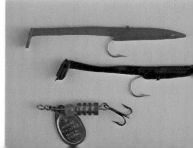

following their every movement. Fishing from a dinghy involves cruising around the periphery of the shoal, never carving through them. The spinner, a little Mepps, or similar lure such as the tiniest spoon, is cast in towards the fish.

The mackerel hit hard and immediately tear off on feeling the resistance to their speed. The light spinning rod bucks and strains as it follows the incredible changes in direction of the fish. The drag will have to be on the lightest setting as few anglers can react to the fish in time to prevent line or tackle breakages.

From the shore, mackerel are capable of a similar fight, even though the addition of a small casting weight is necessary to get the spinner farther from the angler than would be needed when fishing from a boat. The rocky coast that allows fishing over deepish water is often the best location, for the mackerel shoals will approach close in hot weather to find fry. Steep shingle beaches also let the fish come in to the shore but, of course, the casting distances become longer. I've had mackerel on small plugs when the fish were hanging around the rocks. They will stay for a while when the shoal is not big and the food demand too great for the area to hold them. A diving plug, worked in among the creaming froth, where the waves turn at the base of the rocky ledges, is often the place to pick up larger specimens. Offshore, mackerel sometimes hold for a while over pinnacle reefs and broken, rocky ground where the food availability is enough to provide them for a sustaining period. There the mackerel themselves become preyed on by pollack, which produces a frenzied activity that often draws the attention of an even larger predator, the tope, a fierce member of the shark family.

Garfish

Around the mackerel shoals we find garfish, especially in the hotter months of the year. Evidence of their presence can be seen as fish leap from the water, or speed across the surface with their bodies half out of the sea. The shore tackle combination is suitable but the lures must be of the smallest as garfish have a long, delicate bill with a tiny mouth. The hooks must be sharp, for the fish is normally hooked across the bill, which is hard bone with very little purchase even for the sharpest of hook points. Obviously, the tiny baits weigh very little and are not cast easily unless some additional weight is added uptrace. Use just enough lead to make the cast, ensuring that the weight is dull in colour, otherwise you will find garfish striking at the weight.

From an anchored boat, lures can be fluttered in the tide rather than cast. The smallest amount of current stream will turn the blade of a spinner and the lure can be inched across the surface in a way that allows you to see the approach of the gar, like a torpedo. Then the strike and those superb cartwheeling escape tactics follow as the fish feels the tension on the reel line. Both the mackerel and garfish provide some of the finest spinning in saltwater. They deserve the opportunity to show their pace and flashing brilliance so spin light and wisely.

Final Thoughts

There is little difference between spinning techniques and the lures used in fresh or saltwater. There may be far more artificial baits on offer to the freshwater angler but this is due to the influence of American and, latterly, Japanese manufacturers who attempt to satisfy the enormous demand from those markets. Many of the lures used in lakes and rivers will work perfectly well in marine conditions. All they need is added weight to get them down to where the fish are feeding. The size of an artificial lure is decided by two factors: what the fish normally feeds on and the human trait that always suggests a big lure for a big fish.

It is my opinion that the smallest lure will often attract the attention of the larger predators, who are not necessarily seeking a large meal. More often, our baits 'annoy' them or arouse the instinct to strike at things that do not appear appetizing. I believe that the way in which a lure is presented, its action through the water, and selection of a bait suitable for the conditions, are the keys to successful spinning. Trying to duplicate the appearance of a food creature rarely helps. When a lifelike appearance *is* necessary, I spin the natural bait.

There is difficulty in giving a best time for spinning. I could suggest that early morning and late evening, but surely those times must be the best periods for all forms of freshwater fishing. In the sea, things are different. Fish do not seem so governed by the prevailing light. In saltwater the tide is the greatest influence on feeding behaviour, although one of our spinning species, the pollack, swims high in the water at dusk and is taken when it is bent on slashing into packs of fry.

The attraction of spinning as a fishing system is one of mobility and freedom from angling restraints: go seek the predator in its lair, armed with lures that force the fish to attack. With pike, it certainly becomes something personal as you see the swirl, feel the shock of the take and then look into the steely eyes of the fish on the bank. It makes you glad to be bigger than the pike and so aware of its murderous intent.

The pike's cold eyes bring us full circle, back to the reasons for man's love of fishing, back into his prehistoric past when as simple hunter he preyed not only on the creatures of the land but on those that spend their lives under the water . . . Tight Lines!

Right *King of speed! The mackerel is one of the strongest fighting and speediest of swimmers in saltwater. But to get the best sport from this tasty, powerful fish make sure that your tackle is decently balanced to the mackerel's fighting qualities.*

Below *Two contented anglers make their way home under a golden sunset. Their gentle outboard is causing little disturbance to the still water in the quiet of a tranquil evening.*

INDEX

Acknowledgements

Joyce West, Allen Edwards, Michael Shepley, Robin
Prichard and Asjelien Baarslag for those photographs not
taken by the author

Mustad of Norway for the hook illustrations and size chart

Trevor King of Dubery's Fishing Tackle, Hornchurch,
Essex, for fishing tackle

Fred Tamplin, John Woods, Eugene McKeirnan and Francis
McGoldrick for fishing assistance

Christopher Jones for the colour artwork

Len Cacutt for copy editing and advice

Robin L K Wood, for his publishing advice

Goodwin Dorman for design

And all my fishing companions for their help and advice over
many rewarding years